The Little Ones

*A Course of Religious Instruction
for children up to eight years*

and

The Faith for Children

From Seven to Fourteen

by

Mother Mary Eaton
Religious of the Sacred Heart

ST. AUGUSTINE ACADEMY PRESS
HOMER GLEN, ILLINOIS

This volume is a photographic reprint under a single cover
of two individual books written by a single author.

In order to preserve page reference numbers,
the pages in the second book have not been renumbered.

The Little Ones was originally jointly published in 1923
by Sands & Co. in London and
B. Herder Book Company in St. Louis, MO.

This reprinted edition based on the Third Edition
printed in 1930 by Sands & Co.

The Faith for Children was originally published in 1925
by the same.

This reprinted edition based on the 1925 edition.

Imprimaturs for these books can be found
on the reverse of each one's individual title page.

ISBN for this omnibus edition: 978-1-64051-124-8

Mother Mary Eaton

A BRIEF BIOGRAPHICAL SKETCH

Mary Ann Charlotte Eaton (1862-1934) was the daughter of Charles Ormston Eaton, a prominent banker from the East Midlands of England. Just days before her daughter's birth, Mary's mother was received into the Catholic Church, and her father followed three months later. In thanksgiving for the blessing of their conversion, Mary's father sponsored the building of a grand new church in the nearby town of Stamford, while also establishing a chapel in his home at Tolethorpe Hall. The celebration of Mass there marked the first time the Holy Sacrifice had been offered in that part of England since the Reformation.

At the age of 5, Mary suffered a fall that damaged her spine and, despite the best care, she suffered this deformity for the rest of her life. She was often in fragile health, and in 1874, during an illness that brought her to the point of death, she was favored with an apparition of the Blessed Virgin, which she kept a secret the rest of her life. She recovered, and despite the challenges she faced, entered the Roehampton convent of the Society of the Sacred Heart in 1882. This marked the beginning of a long career as a teacher, not only in the convent boarding schools, but most especially in the teacher training schools of the Society.

Her infirmity was an aid to her in humility as well as perseverance, and she was always revered for her patience and inspired teaching. It was when she was stationed at the Society's schools in Edinburgh that she was asked by the editor of a journal published in Birmingham (where her brother, Fr. Robert Ormston Eaton, was a well-known and widely published priest of the Oratory), to commit her teaching methods to book form. This resulted in the books *The Little Ones*, *The Faith for Children*, *Consider the Child*, *Our Inheritance*, *Our Birthright*, and *The Bible Beautiful*, all of which she intended as suggestions for the students, to help develop a sense of personal initiative in learning the faith.

In 1934, her health began to deteriorate quickly, and in March she suffered a stroke which left her bedridden. She died on May 8 and was buried in the newly established cemetery at the convent in Kilgraston.

THE LITTLE ONES

THE LITTLE ONES

A Course of Religious Instruction for children up to eight years

By

MARY EATON

Religious of the Sacred Heart

ST. AUGUSTINE ACADEMY PRESS
HOMER GLEN, ILLINOIS

Nihil Obstat

GEORGIUS CANONICUS MULLAN,
Censor Deputatus.

Imprimatur

✠ HENRICUS
Epus. Tipasit.

Edimburgi,
die XI Aug., 1925.

May this book help some of those whose privilege it is to prepare God's way in the hearts of His little ones.

Training College,
Craiglockhart.

Feast of the Holy Innocents, 1922.

CONTENTS

THIRD YEAR

THE LITTLE ONES

I. GOD MADE ME

1. Appeal to eyes, ears, fingers, etc., and ask : " Who gave them to Baby ? "
God our Father, Who is in heaven, gave them : He made them.

God gave you ten fingers and ten toes, two legs and two arms, two eyes, etc.—that is the way God made you.

You have brown hair and *you* black hair— *you* have blue eyes and *you* have grey, because that is what God gave to each of you.

God made our eyes to open and to shut; when God makes it dark we go to sleep, and we shut our eyes; when God makes it light again, He wakes us up, and we open our eyes again.

You can do many things : you can laugh— you can sing—you can talk—you can dance— you can clap your hands—(make the babies do some of these actions)—because God made you able to do all these things. (Develop).

2. Show the children gold-fish or tadpoles

in a glass bowl—or a canary—or a kitten—
or any young thing full of life.

Let them admire and play with it. Then
say and get them to say—"God made it."

Repeat, with flowers of many colours :
God made the rain that the flower drinks—
God made the sun that warms the flower—
God made the blue sky—God made every-
thing.

Only God can make the birds to fly—the
fish to swim—the kitten to play—the flowers
to grow and smell sweet. He made them and
everything else too.

We make things out of something He has
made and given to us. He makes things with
nothing. He simply wanted you and you
were made. (Develop).

God made our hearts—we love Father and
Mother with all our heart—we love God with
all our heart—God gave us our hearts to love
Him with.

God made your souls too—He put your
soul inside you—He loves your soul—He
loves it so much that He lives in it. It is
His own little home, where He lives. If you
talk to God inside your heart, you will find
Him there.

3. When we make something it belongs to
us.

God made me, therefore I belong to God.
(Develop).

When God made me, He did so because He wanted me—He wanted me for something— What is that something?

He wants me to love Him—that is why He gave me my heart.

He wants me to do what He likes—not always what *I* like.

He likes me to do what I am told.

He likes me to be kind and gentle.

He likes me sometimes to talk to Him. (Develop).

He wants me, and He made me to live here for a long time, doing what He wants—and then some day He means to take me to live with Him in a lovely place, where He will give me everything *I* want for ever

II. THE SIGN OF THE CROSS

1. Show the children a fairly large Crucifix and get them to repeat: " Jesus loves me. Jesus died for me."

2. Tell them that because Jesus died on the Cross, He loves the Cross and we love it too, and He loves us to make a cross to show that we love it. Would they like to make a cross?

Show them how to make it, using of course your left hand and touching your right shoulder first—leave out the words till they know how to make the Sign.

3. Then make the Sign on the Crucifix, with the words.

Touch the sacred Head of Our Lord and say : " In the Name of the Father "—His Feet and add : " and of the Son "—His Left Hand—" and of the Holy "—His Right Hand —" Ghost "—His Heart—"Amen."

Do not attempt any explanation of the words. Doing it on the Crucifix connects the Sign of the Cross with the Passion, and this is enough for the present. The children practise making it at first without the words.

You should make it on yourself very often and sometimes on the Crucifix.

Give no details of the Passion as yet—only, " Jesus loves me—He died for me on the Cross." They will not understand fully, of course, but that does not matter—the very words have power and they will be happy making crosses.

THE SIGN OF THE CROSS. (Story)

Object. To familiarise the children with the words. Each time you repeat the words, " Sign of the Cross," make it, saying the words very slowly.

Once upon a time there were two children, who lived near a big wood. One day they were out in the wood when a storm came on. The rain poured down, the wind blew, and it made such a noise, that both Willie and Margaret were very much afraid. Willie made the Sign of the Cross. (We will all make it with him). In the Name, etc.

"What are you doing, Willie?" asked Margaret.

"I am making the Sign of the Cross," said Willie.

"Why do you do that?" asked Margaret.

"Because I am afraid of the storm," said Willie.

"So am I; but why do you make that Cross?"

"Because that Cross will save me from the storm and from all harm. It will conquer the wind and the rain, it will conquer everything." And he made it again. (In the Name, etc.)

Margaret, who was younger than Willie did not quite understand, but she believed everything Willie said and she began to make the Sign of the Cross too. (In the Name, etc.), and then she asked:

"Is the Cross really as strong as that, and will it really save us from the storm?"

"Yes," said Willie, and just at that moment the wind gave a great howl and he made the Sign of the Cross again. (In the Name, etc.)

Margaret did so too, for she was more frightened even than Willie.

"What do those words mean?" she asked.

"They mean, 'God bless me,'" said Willie,

and as he said it, a big tree gave such a loud crack that both Willie and Margaret made the Sign of the Cross again together. (In the Name, etc.)

"God bless me," said Margaret.

"And me too," said Willie.

The wind seemed to get louder and louder, and the big tree that cracked could not hold up any longer against the storm and it fell with a great crash.

"God bless us," said Willie, and both he and Margaret made the sign of the Cross again. (In the Name, etc.)

"If it had not been for the Sign of the Cross, we should both have been killed."

And just at that moment the wind began to blow more softly, and the rain stopped, and the sun came out, and Willie and Margaret soon got back safely home, for they had not far to go. But Margaret never forgot what Willie had taught her and very often after that, especially when she was frightened about anything, she used to make the Sign of the Cross. (In the Name, etc.), and say: "God bless Willie and me."

III. GOD MADE EVERYTHING

God did not only make me: He made all the other little boys and girls in this room—in this town, and all over the world—all the big men and women too—and everything else in the world.

Get the children to give as long a list as they can—supplement and suggest.

Get them to go over some of the big pictures used in conversational lessons, and ask them, as each object is named : Who made it ?

Distribute pictures of animals, flowers, children, men and women, and keep each child busy looking at them and repeating softly : " God made *you* and *you* and *you*."

(A good many pictures are required for this, but they are very easily collected from newspapers and magazines—without cost. If pasted on some kind of linen they last much longer and they make a lesson of this kind easier and more attractive.)

Give a lesson on, *e.g.*, " Birds," just as an ordinary conversational lesson—only make the whole turn on God.

God made the bird with its pretty feathers and soft breast ; God made the twigs and the wool and the straw for its nest ; God made its pretty blue eggs ; God loves the little bird, He takes care of it, He gives it food ; He made the trees for it to build its nest in. God made the little bird sing. God knows I like to hear the bird sing, so He made the bird as a present for me, etc.

ANGELS I.

1. We have seen that God made everybody—you and me and all other people in the world.

I am going to tell you to-day about some beautiful people He made to live with Him in Heaven, whom we cannot yet see, but who can see us, and who love us very much—they are called Angels.

(Show picture of Guardian Angel—describe brightly—dwell on the gentle face—the white sparkling robe—the beautiful strong wings). Heaven is a long way from here—up in the blue sky—but they, in a second, can fly from Heaven to earth and back again.

2. Now I must tell you a wonderful thing —God knew when He put us in this world that we should want someone to look after us—Father and Mother were not enough, because they could not always be with us— so—just fancy! when a little boy or girl comes into this world, God sends for one of these bright Angels and says—"My little child (give name of one of the class) has just arrived in that home, down there on the earth, and you, my Angel, are to look after him for Me. Take great care of him—see that he does not hurt himself, and try and keep his soul as white and pure as it is now— every day he lives and when he comes to die,

bring him back to Me, that he may live with
Me and with you in our bright Heaven.

Then the Angel God has chosen smiles very
brightly (for Angels love doing something for
God), and he flies down to earth and stands
over that happy little boy or girl, and loves
him and takes care of him.

Just think, there are—say—40 little children here, and each one has his own dear
Angel to look after him. I told you we cannot see the Angels—we cannot see the fairies
or the air in the room either—but our Angel
is here, keeping away what might harm us
and praying for us, and though it is a pity
we cannot see him (refer back to picture) we
can talk to him, and if we listen carefully,
he will sometimes talk to us. We shall not
hear his voice but we shall know what he
wants to tell us.

When we feel naughty we think of our
Angel at our side, and we say : " What does
Jesus want me to do ?" and the Angel tells
us.

When we are cross we say : " Dear Angel,
I feel so cross—make me good," and he will
help us to be good : and often we say : " Dear
Angel, you are good to me : I love you."

3. I will tell you a story, which will show
you how much we must love our Guardian
Angel.

Once upon a time there was an old man

B

who lived with his wife and son in a country far away from here. He was a very good old man, but he was blind, and this made him very sad. One day he called his son, who was called Tobias, and said to him : "Go and do what I tell you—I am very poor, but there is a rich man who lives far away from here who owes me a great deal of money —you must go to him and ask him to help us. This made Tobias sad too, because he did not know the way to the home of the rich man, but his father told him to find someone who would show him the way.

So Tobias went out, and who do you think he saw standing just outside the door? . . . A beautiful young man, quite ready to take a walk. And Tobias asked him who he was.

Now I must tell you a secret. The young man did not tell Tobias who he really was— because God did not want Tobias to know just then, but it was—it truly, truly was— Tobias's Guardian Angel !

You see, God loved Tobias and his poor old blind father, and He knew that Tobias would have to go a long way to get the money, and that his Guardian Angel would help him very much. And so it was that Tobias and his dog, who was very fond of him, and who would not be left behind, and the Guardian Angel, all set out together— and they came to a big river—and a great big fish jumped out of the river on to Tobias, and it was just going to eat him up, when Tobias called out to his Guardian Angel (only he did not know it was his Guardian Angel) : " Help me ! Help me !" And his Guardian Angel said : " Take hold of the fish and don't be afraid !" and Tobias did as he was told, and he caught the fish and killed it, and cooked it. So after all, it was Tobias who ate the fish, and the wicked fish did not touch Tobias, and all because he did what his Guardian Angel told him !

After that they got to the house where the man was who owed the money. And Tobias found there a beautiful Princess, whose name was Sara, and he married her and they were very happy. And the Guardian Angel stayed with Tobias all this time ; and at last they remembered the poor old, blind father, and Tobias thought he had better go back home again, because he knew that his father would be very sad without him. So they set out— Tobias and Sara and the Guardian Angel and the little dog, and they all got home quite safe. But the little dog was so glad to be at home again, and ran on so quickly that he got there first, and by barking, jumping and wagging his tail, he told the old man who was coming. And the poor old blind father began to run too to meet his son, and he gave his hand to a man who was standing near, because he was afraid of falling, and he went to meet Tobias. Then he and Tobias and Sara the Princess, and the Guardian Angel, all thanked God and were very happy.

But that was not all, for the Guardian Angel told Tobias to put some stuff on his father's eyes, and he did so, and the old man gave a great cry, saying: "I bless Thee, O Lord," and he was no longer blind but could see quite well with his two eyes just as well as you can.

They made a great feast, which lasted seven days, and when it was over, suddenly Tobias saw the young man who had been so kind and done so much for him all this time, now changed into a beautiful Angel, with lovely wings, which he had kept hidden all the time, so that Tobias never even guessed that he was an Angel; and the Angel said to him: " Peace be to you, for I must now go back to Heaven, but bless God and tell everybody how good He is."

And Tobias tried to thank the Guardian Angel, but he flew back to Heaven, and Tobias could see him no more, but he knew that though he could not see him, he would come back again, and he never forgot his wonderful Guardian Angel, but he loved him all his life.   And Tobias and Sara and the old father, no longer blind, but seeing with his two eyes, and the little dog, lived happily till they were too old to live any more, and then they too went to Heaven.

Now this is a truly true story.

ANGELS II.

If we could each have a pair of wings, strong enough to carry us anywhere, where would *you* like to fly to?

(Get answers).

It would be great fun: let us pretend:

I am going to fly up and up till I get to Heaven: that is the beautiful place where God lives.

I am going to pay a little visit and then fly back again. Who will come with me?

Now we must shut our eyes tight and fancy we are going up, up, up through the blue sky! . . . Ah! what is that? Why I declare there are two beautiful gates—not shut—wide open.

. . . And who is that? What a beautiful Angel! (Show picture). He is all white and his wings are glistening—he looks gentle and kind—let us speak to him!

" Dear Angel—we are earth-children, and we have shut our eyes tight, and we thought we were flying up—up—up, so high till we reached these beautiful gates. Please, will you tell us if this is Heaven?

The Angel shakes his head—"No," he says, "this is not Heaven—only a beautiful place, where earth-children may come, whenever they are tired, and talk to the Angels, and ask them any question they like."

So now, we can ask our Guardian Angel any questions we like.

I am going to begin : "Please, dear Angel, are there many Angels in Heaven?"

And the Angel says : "Yes, a great, great many : all shining, and bright and beautiful."

"Please, dear Angel, is Heaven a beautiful place?"

And the Angel answers : "Yes, so beautiful, that only beautiful people are let in."

"Please, dear Angel, what shall I do when I get to Heaven?"

And the Angel says : "The thing you like best, all day long, and it is always day in Heaven."

"Please, dear Angel, whom shall I see in Heaven?"

And the Angel's wings tremble, and he bows his head, and he says in a low voice : "GOD." . . .

Is not that wonderful, children?

(If possible, get the little ones to ask questions; if none are forthcoming, go straight on, but to provoke questions should be one of our chief aims in all this teaching).

There is another Angel (picture); how busy

he is! See, he is gathering roses. Shall I tell you why?

When little earth-children say a wee prayer, the Angels hear them, and sometimes our Guardian Angel—sometimes another Angel catches it up and turns it into a lovely rose, and he flies off with it to Heaven, to offer it to Baby Jesus. And of all the roses that are offered to Jesus, the ones he likes best are those that the Angels have taken from the lips of little children like you.

So be quite sure to say some little prayers to Baby Jesus every day.

See, here is another Angel, but he is flying down from Heaven to earth. I wonder what he is carrying? He has got something in his arms: what do you think it is? Can you guess? (Obtain some guesses).

Now, I will tell you: he is going to some little children, who are sick and in bed, and in pain, and he is carrying them each a happy dream, sent to them by Baby Jesus to make them forget their pain and have a nice, quiet sleep.

I will tell you one of these dreams, that came straight from Heaven and was carried by Angels.

It was not sent to a sick little child, but to a poor, weary man, who had to take a long journey. It was sent by God long, long ago, and the man's name was Jacob.

He had to go into a country he had never seen before, and he walked and walked and walked all through the day, and yet, when evening came, he had not got to the place he wanted to go to. But he was very tired and it began to get quite dark; so he said to himself: "I cannot walk any more; I am too tired, I must lie down and go to sleep."

He had no nice bed to lie down on, so he took some hard stones that he found on the road and put them under his head instead of a pillow and . . . he fell fast asleep.

And God was sorry for him because he had walked so far and was so tired, so He sent His Angels to give him a beautiful dream. (Just like the Angel we saw just now, who was carrying dreams to the little sick children).

This was the dream God sent Jacob when he was asleep, after having walked so far.

Jacob saw in his sleep a ladder. (Draw one on B.B.). It was such a big ladder: its foot was on the earth like this one, but it went up and up right through the blue sky (as we wanted to do) . . . until the top of the ladder reached heaven. And who do you think was on the ladder?

Why, Angels of course: some going up from earth to Heaven, carrying gifts from earth-children to God—others coming down all the way from Heaven to earth, bringing God's gifts to earth.

It was a beautiful dream, and Jacob loved it—the Angels were so bright, and when he woke he thanked God, and found that he was not even one little bit tired, so he went on his journey again and arrived at the place he wanted to go to.

So you see, it is quite easy for the Angels to go from Heaven to earth and from earth to Heaven. They can fly if they like, or if they like the ladder better, they can go by it instead.

THE ANNUNCIATION

We have seen how beautiful Angels are— how we each have a Guardian Angel to take care of us, and how there are many, many Angels in Heaven.

Not all of these are Guardian Angels, but all of them are busy doing what God wants them to do. Some of these Angels are very great Princes in Heaven, and to-day I am going to tell you what happened to one of these Princes long, long ago, the most wonderful thing that has ever happened in this world.

But first I want you to remember that God often sends His Angels down with a message from Him : sometimes it is a dream, like the one he sent to Jacob, sometimes it is to tell His earth-children something that He wants them to know.

Well, many, many years ago, God called one of the great Prince-Angels and gave him a message to take to earth.

(If the children do not know what a message means, make them take a few from you to the class and from the class to you).

When the great Prince-Angel, whose name was Gabriel, had heard what God said, he bowed very low, and all the other Angels' wings trembled, and they bowed too, for it was such a wonderful message.

And Gabriel did what God told him, and flew straight from Heaven to earth, and he never stopped anywhere till he came to the little town to which God had sent him.

In this little town there was a little street, where in a little house lived a very beautiful maiden, and her name was Mary. She was fifteen years old—she was poor, and she was so holy that the great Prince-Angel bowed before her and said : " Hail, full of grace !"

Mary was a little frightened at first, not at the sight of the great Angel, for that made her very glad, but at what he said.

But Gabriel told her not to fear, because God was pleased with her, and had sent him to her, to ask her to be the Mother of God.

" To be the Mother of God !" that was such a wonderful thing that again Mary wondered and asked : " How can this be ?" But Gabriel told her it was God Who was to do this thing—God Who can do all things—everything—and Mary saw that God wanted her to say " yes," and so she answered : " Be it done to me, as you have said."

And the Angel bowed again, because Mary, who had been chosen to be Mother of God, was, he knew, to be some day Queen of Angels too; and then, full of joy, he flew straight back to Heaven, where all the other Angels came out to meet him. " Good news," he cried : " Good news, for heaven—good news for earth !" And as soon as he was gone, Mary fell upon her knees and whispered : " God—God—God !"

She knew now what the Angel meant : God loved us all so much that He wanted to send His only Son to live on this earth just as we do. He wanted Him to come as a little baby —just as each of you came on to this earth, and He wanted Mary to be the Mother of His little Baby Son, and She had said She would.

Follow this story up on the following day, by showing the children a big picture of the Annunciation, and getting them to recognise Our Lady and the Angel, and to tell you what they remember of the story.

Talk to them about Our Lady, and get them to ask questions : your chief object is to get the little ones to realise that She loves them, and then that they love Her.

Tell them in as many different ways as possible that the Baby Jesus and Mother Mary love them—that we must love them too. How much ? Open your arms a little : " So much ?" They open their arms by degrees till they are stretched out wide : " So much."

An explanation of the well-known picture : " The breadth of My Love " would be an excellent way of ending this lesson, but the idea alone is suitable, not the name.

V.   THE JOURNEY TO BETHLEHEM*
(Story and Play)

Not long after the beautiful Angel had left holy Mary, one day there came a knock at the door of the little house, in the little street, and a proud, rough-looking man came in with some big papers in his hand. He did not speak to our dear Lady as the Angel had done, and he did not bow low, but he told her in a rude way, that she was to leave the little town where she was, and go to Bethlehem. (Bethlehem was the name of the town, just as . . . is the name of the town where we live).

Bethlehem was some way off, but the King

* Luke ii., 1-6.

from whom the rough man came, had ordered everybody to go to Bethlehem, and write their names in a big book, so that the King might count them up and see how many people there were altogether.

You remember that Mary had promised to be the Mother of Baby Jesus, and it was in Bethlehem that Baby Jesus was to be born. Holy Mary knew this, so she was not surprised at the rude man's message.

Now there lived in the little house where Mary lived Mary's husband—a great Saint—whose name was Joseph—He took great care of Mary, because God had told him to, and he loved her very much, and an Angel had told him that Baby Jesus was coming, and that he was to take great care of Him too.

When St. Joseph heard the rough man's message he answered that both he and Mary would go straight to Bethlehem, and then the rough man went away and slammed the door after him.

Both Mary and Joseph began at once to get ready. They were very poor, and all they had to take with them was a donkey (show picture), on which Our Lady rode, and a little bundle of clothes, for Mary and St. Joseph and Baby Jesus, when He came.

And now would you like to go with Mary and Joseph to Bethlehem, where Baby Jesus was to be born?

Get the children to march two by two round the room, to music.

One represents Our Lady, another St. Joseph, and these go first and wear some distinctive mark.

A few of the children go to one side of the room, e.g. by B.B.—representing the inhabitants of Bethlehem.

When the march has lasted long enough, they reach Bethlehem.

St. Joseph knocks against the wall, or against B.B. etc., and says: " May we come in ?" and each of the Bethlehemites answers in turn : " No room : no room :"

Mary and Joseph, followed by the rest of the children, go away very sad.

VI. THE NATIVITY

Preparation. Conversational Lesson during the week, on an Ox. Pictures and a rough sketch of the cave on brown paper or on B.B.

The cave is empty except for the Manger (teach word and thing) and the straw. Give some straw to the children.

For all the coming work, a Crib is badly needed.

A pretty, devotional one can easily be made at practically no cost.

1. Procure a packing-case of convenient

size. Stand the case on its side on a board, large enough to give a border all round, about six inches wide. Nail the case to the board.

2. Take 2 oz. of Vandyke brown powder paint, and a penny packet of size. Dissolve the size in half-a-pint of boiling water, and mix the paint.

Paint the packing-case inside and out, and the border as well.

3. Procure some bits of bark off an old tree. Nail or glue these to the sides and top of the Crib.

4. Put some bits of clinkers and cinders on to the sides of the Crib, and also on the border at the back. Fill up the holes between them with putty, and put bits of yew and evergreen into the putty.

5. Cover the foreground with thick size or glue. Throw down dried moss and bits of gravel on to this, and press it down with your hands.

6. Procure a devotional coloured print of the Nativity, the figures to be in proportion to the size of your crib. Cut out the Figures of Our Lady, St. Joseph and the Holy Child, also the Manger, the Ox and the Ass. Paste them on to stiffish cardboard and put them under a flat weight. In every case, let the cardboard at the base of the Figure protrude about a couple of inches.

When the Figures are dry, bend these two

inches of cardboard back and fasten the Figures in position, inside the crib, with drawing-pins.

If a back support is also necessary, one can easily be made of a flap of cardboard, but if the cardboard is fairly stiff, the Figures will stand quite well without.

The Shepherds and the Kings, the Star, etc., should be added as required.

A pretty room, which can be used for e.g. the Annunciation, the Last Supper, the marriage Feast of Cana, etc., etc., can easily be made in the same way as the above, and will be found useful and effective.

THE STORY OF THE NATIVITY*

Link up with the last lesson by reminding the children how they went to Bethlehem with Mary and Joseph, and tried to find room for them. What did all the people answer?

Then continue the story.

The night came on, it was winter time and cold and dark, white snow was on the ground, and only the stars seemed bright and happy; they were twinkling overhead as if they were sending a secret message to one another, but no one noticed them: if only people had listened they would have heard the secret: " Baby Jesus is coming, Baby Jesus is com-

*Luke ii., 6, 7.

ing." But no one paid any attention, and poor St. Joseph, who had charge of our dear Lady Mary, and who was to take care of Baby Jesus when He came, became very sad, because everyone was so rude and went on saying : " No room, no room." If only *you* had been there, you could have given your room, and your little bed to Baby Jesus, but everyone was so busy, and there were so many people in Bethlehem already, that there was no room, no room. What was St. Joseph to do ?

Just at that moment a man came up and seeing Our Lady sitting on a bench—he did not know who She was, only that She looked very tired—he asked St. Joseph what he wanted.

St. Joseph told him that he wanted a room for the night, but the man answered just as the others had done : " No room, no room !" but then he added : " There is a cave behind my house, where I keep my ox ; you can have that for the night, if you like."

It was just like the cave you saw in the picture (put picture up again), and though it was indeed a poor place for Our Lady and St. Joseph and Baby Jesus, who was coming, St Joseph thanked the man and went back to fetch the ass which he had left in the town and he fastened him up, just near the ox.

He made Our Lady sit down for She was

C

very tired, and then he swept and tidied the cave, after he had lit the little lamp he had brought with him.

Our Lady asked him to put the manger by Her side for Baby Jesus, who was coming, and St. Joseph filled it full of fresh straw and placed it by Her.

Then he went to the front of the cave and looked out and watched for Baby Jesus. The stars were still twinkling and whispering their secret and St. Joseph listened and heard them saying: " Baby Jesus is coming! Baby Jesus is coming!"

The big bell in Bethlehem was still booming: " No room! No room!" but all the little bells on the hills were tinkling so softly and so sweetly: "Baby Jesus is coming! Baby Jesus is coming!" And the great white Angel, who had first brought the wonderful message, flew through the air on his strong bright wings and stood over the cave and he too sang: " Baby Jesus is coming! Baby Jesus is coming!" And St. Joseph fell on his knees and prayed, for he knew that Baby Jesus was God.

And all was quite silent for a moment: the stars stopped whispering and the bells stopped tinkling and the big Angel stopped singing and a bright golden light filled the cave and Baby Jesus came. . . .

And Our Lady took Him in Her arms and kissed Him and loved Him and laid Him in the manger on the straw.

VII. THE NATIVITY

The children might begin by going in procession to the Crib, singing:

> Come, come, come to the Manger,
> Children come, to the children's King,
> Sing, sing, sweet band of Angels,
> Stars of morning o'er Bethlehem sing.
> (*Arundel Collection*, No. 43, trans. by Fr. Caswell.)

Then they all gather round the Crib and repeat several times: "Baby Jesus I love You," and something else of their own, just as each one likes; let them return to their places singing.

Whilst the whole class is occupied with some kind of handwork, take groups of eight or ten at a time, to pay visits to the crib. They are going to talk to Baby Jesus and to do something for Him, *e.g.* smooth the straw or straighten the yew, etc. Make the visit as simple as possible—a talk to Baby Jesus and Holy Mary about themselves or about their homes or about Bethlehem, ending with: "Baby Jesus, bless us," and the Sign of the Cross.

They should each make up something to say to Baby Jesus of their own.

VIII. THE SECOND HALF OF THE HAIL MARY

Show a picture of Our Lady with the Infant Jesus on Her knee.

(As well as one big picture, it is often a help to distribute small coloured pictures among the class, so that every two children see one quite close. They must be taught to treat them reverently.)

Get the babies to say who the beautiful Lady is—Mary—Holy Mary. And who is Her little Son? Jesus—Baby Jesus.

(Call Our Lady " Holy Mary " throughout the lesson, for the sake of repetition.)

Holy Mary is the Mother of Baby Jesus and Baby Jesus is God—Holy Mary is the Mother of God.

"Holy Mary, Mother of God!" She likes us to call Her that. She is smiling and asking Baby Jesus to bless us.

Let us say it again, very softly : " Holy Mary, Mother of God, pray for us."

Let six go together and kneel at the Crib and say : " Holy Mary, Mother of God, pray for us ;" (till the whole class has been).

I wonder if She is praying for us *now?* Yes, She is ! Look at your picture and tell Her you know She is praying for us *Now*.

" Holy Mary, Mother of God, pray for us

sinners, *Now.*" Lay no stress on the word
" sinners." Children of five are not sinners.
In the same way, no stress need be made on
the words, " at the hour of our death." They
can be taught by repetition, as in a story,
like the following, or otherwise.

A STORY TO TEACH THE WORDS OF THE SECOND HALF OF THE HAIL MARY

Once upon a time there were three brothers,
their names were Francis, Antony, and Bernard.

One day, when they were out walking, they
came to a spot where three roads met, and
they saw in front of them a little Angel. Where
he stood a sunbeam had fallen and it made
him look quite golden.

" Where are you going, Francis ?" said the
Angel.

Francis thought for a moment; he had
never been spoken to by an Angel before, at
least if he had he did not remember it; but
he answered quite nicely : " Dear Angel, I
was going down the road to the right, but I
think now, I should like to go with you
instead."

" Not just yet," said the Angel, " and
Antony, where are you going to ?"

" Dear Angel, I was going down the road to the left, but I will go wherever you tell me."

" Very good," said the Angel, " and Bernard, where are you going to ?"

Bernard answered : " Dear Angel, I was going to keep on the road I am on now, but I will go wherever you say."

" That is quite right," said the Angel, " now listen. I have been sent to you by Holy Mary," and as the Angel said Holy Mary's name his wings seemed to tremble with brightness, and he bowed his head and looked so happy, because She was his Queen. " She has sent me to tell you to come to Her Palace. There She is waiting for you. So go straight on along the middle of the road, and whenever you want help say the ' Holy Mary.' If you do that you will get to the Palace of the Queen."

And as the little Angel said the last words, he spread his wings and was gone, and the sunbeam went with him.

The three brothers started on their journey —they were very grateful to the Angel, but he had flown away so quickly that they had not had time to say " Thank you."

They had not gone very far when they heard the howling of a wolf, and they were all three, very much afraid.

" Holy Mary, Mother of God," said Bernard.

" Pray for us sinners," said Francis.

" Now and at the hour of our death," said
Antony.

They said it three times (repeat) and at the
third time the howling had stopped, and the
wolf had trotted off to find his dinner somewhere else.

On they went, thanking "Holy Mary"
very much, but soon after that they came to
a deep river. There was nothing but water in
front of them and no bridge across. They did
not know how to swim, so there was nothing
to be done but to say "Holy Mary" over
again.

" Holy Mary, Mother of God," said Bernard.

" Pray for us sinners," said Francis.

" Now and at the hour of our death, Amen,"
said Antony.

This time they went on saying it, over and
over again (repeat). Still no boat came to
fetch them and the water seemed to get deeper
and deeper and it cut straight across the road.

" Suppose we went round by this wood ?"
said Antony.

" No," said Francis, " the Angel said we
were to keep straight on."

" We have not said 'Holy Mary' often
enough," said Bernard. And he began again :
" Holy Mary, Mother of God."

" Pray for us sinners," said Francis.

" Now and at the hour of our death," said
Antony.

Suddenly they saw at the opposite side of the river a golden sunbeam, and a minute later, the little Angel was standing on it beckoning to them to come across.

"Holy Mary, Mother of God," said Bernard, and he plunged into the river.

"Pray for us sinners," said Francis, as he tumbled into the water after him.

"Now and at the hour of our death," said Antony, who could not bear to be left behind.

How they got to the opposite side they never knew, but somehow or other they found themselves quite safely there, and their clothes were not even wet!

Holy Mary and the little Angel knew all about it, you may be sure. But when they looked round the little Angel flew away and the sunbeam went after him.

On they went along the road as before, wondering what would happen next and hoping they would see the beautiful Palace soon, but there was no sign of it and they were getting very tired, and once they all but stopped. What would have happened if they had, I cannot tell, for the Angel had told them to go on without stopping. So instead of stopping they said "Holy Mary" again (repeat), and after that they did not feel so tired.

Just then Antony touched Bernard's arm and said: "Look!" and Francis almost shouted, "Oh, look!" and Bernard jumped,

and he too said : "Look !" for there in front
of them, sparkling in the bright sun, stood the
most beautiful Palace they had ever dreamt of.
There were lovely gates in front, all bright
shining gold, and strong tall towers, made of
silver, glittering with diamonds on either side
of the gates, and at the top of each tower stood
a beautiful tall Angel with folded wings,
watching and guarding the Palace of the
Queen.

"Holy Mary, Mother of God, let us in,"
said Bernard.

"That is not what you must say," said
Francis.

"Holy Mary, Mother of God, pray for us
sinners."

"Now and at the hour of our death, Amen,"
said Antony.

And as they said it, the two tall Angels
flew from the Towers to the Gates, one with
white wings, the other with blue, bearing in
their arms a beautiful Cross. They touched
the Gates with the Cross, and the golden gates
flew open, and there was their own little Angel
standing in his sunbeam, and as they looked
the sunbeam grew longer and longer till it
reached the spot where Bernard, Francis and
Antony were kneeling and they saw then that
the sunbeam was really a golden ladder, and
the little Angel beckoned and they all three
ran up the golden steps, on and on, higher

and higher, until at last, they reached the beautiful room, where Holy Mary was.

And the golden gates shut behind them and the two Angels kept watch on the Towers as before.

IX. The SHEPHERDS*

1. Tell the story of the shepherds—who they were—give them names—introduce several little shepherd boys among them.

2. What they were doing—watching—looking after some of the sheep—sleeping—keeping up fire—its red light, etc.

3. Suddenly an Angel stood close by, on grass—describe.

4. " Fear not—go to Bethlehem—there you will find Baby Jesus and Holy Mary." (The Gospel words are too difficult.)

5. Rows of Angels in the sky—describe each row, in a different colour. The lovely singing : " Joy ! Joy ! Joy in Heaven and on earth. Peace and Joy !" †

6. The Shepherds' conversation : " Let us go and see Baby Jesus and Holy Mary."

7. They come with their sheep and lambs. What Holy Mary and St. Joseph say to them.

* Luke ii., 8-18.

† Nelson's Bible Wall Pictures " The Angel Choir " No. 140.   Price unmounted 8d. each : with a metal rim at top and bottom 1s. 9d. each.

DRAMATISATION

1. Divide the class into Angels, Shepherds and Sheep.

Sheep learn to ba-a-a-a.

The Shepherds say it is very cold and gather round the fire: (an inverted stool, with a bit of red paper on it.) They wonder why the stars are so bright. Angel appears.

(An Angel's dress is very quickly manufactured out of two bits of an old muslin curtain, on a little white foundation. Throw one bit, twice the length of the child's height, over one shoulder and the other bit, over the other. Let the muslin fall quite freely; no stitching, merely a pin to keep the muslin over shoulders. A pair of paper wings completes the whole).

The Angel says: "Go to Bethlehem: Holy Mary and Baby Jesus want you."

The Shepherds fall on their knees.

The other Angels appear, standing on a low bench. Help them to sing:

> "List a secret we would tell,
> God has come with you to dwell."

or simply: "Joy, joy! Peace and Joy!" or any other very simple words.

Scene II. THE SHEPHERDS GO TO THE CAVE

1. The Angels go first and kneel round it.
2. The Shepherds talk a little about

(a) Angels (b) what they said: (c) what it means. They make up their minds to go to the cave.

3. They go there, two by two, singing: "Come, come, come to the Manger" or anything else preferred. The Sheep follow very quietly.

They can bring paper toys or anything else they like as presents for Baby Jesus. They lay these down in front of the Crib and say:

> "All our love to You we bring,
> Take it, bless us little King!"

or any other prayer. "Jesus, we love You," repeated several times, is a very good one.

X. THE STORY OF THE WISE MEN*

1. Just about the time when Baby Jesus was born, there lived far away from Bethlehem, three very Wise Men. They were very rich, as well as very wise, and best of all, they were very good.

These three Wise Men were very fond of looking at the stars; and every evening when it began to grow dark the three Wise Men would go out-of-doors and stand watching for the stars to come out too. They never had to wait very long before first one star and then another and then a great number would shine out quite brightly, and the three Wise Men

* Matt. ii., 1-12.

tried to find out all they could about them.
The stars seemed to tell them a great deal
about God and about the beautiful things He
had made, and the three Wise Men grew wiser
and wiser every day.

One day they went out as usual to watch
for the stars, when suddenly, without any
warning, there stood flashing in the sky a most
beautiful star—far more beautiful than any
the three Wise Men had seen before. It was
of a lovely deep blue colour, and it sent out
such long rays of light that they fell on the
hearts of the three Wise Men, and made them
love God. "What does it mean?" said the
first Wise Man.

"What can it mean?" said the second Wise
Man.

"Let us wait and see," said the third Wise
Man, and he was the wisest of them all. So
they all three waited and watched and
wondered. Now this Star was Baby Jesus's
own star, and the three Wise Men knew that
some day Baby Jesus was to come, and this
beautiful star told them that He had come,
and that He wanted the three Wise Men to
come to His Court.

This message made the three Wise Men
very glad, and they at once set out on their
journey, and Baby Jesus's Star travelled on
in front of them and sent its long bright rays
down on the path they were to follow.

Tell in story form: (a) The journey and arrival at the city of a wicked king.

(b) Their stay in the city: " Where is He, the Baby King? Where was He born?" (The children will love being able to answer this question).

(c) Their arrival at Bethlehem and the offering of the presents to the Great King, Baby Jesus. (Describe the reappearance of Baby Jesus's Star, very dramatically.) Show a coloured print of Burne Jones's picture: " The Star of Bethlehem."

The story of the Epiphany lends itself easily to dramatisation, and a great deal can be made out of the three gifts the children each choose to take with them for the Baby King.

Not more than a word need be said about the killing of little children by the wicked king: it was very sad, but the little ones were glad to die for Baby Jesus, and He has given them a beautiful Heaven ever since!

The flight into Egypt can be told in simple story form or left till next year.

Play: A MOMENT OF SILENCE TO LISTEN FOR THE CHILD JESUS

1. Obtain from the children that real " immobility " of which Madame Montessori speaks in her " Handbook."

Show the children how to sit absolutely still, " with feet still, body still, arms still, head still."

2. Either half-darken the room or get the children to close their eyes. Teach them how to listen for all the little sounds which they can hear in the absolute silence : and then say : " I'll be Our Lady and call you one by one."

3. Go behind the Crib and whisper each name, so softly that the child has to listen attentively to hear it.

When called, he rises and finds his way to the crib : he must walk so lightly as to make no noise, and when he reaches the Crib he says the Holy Name very softly. When they are thus all round the Crib, make them sing something to the Infant Jesus.

The passage in Madame Montessori's Handbook, of which this is an adaptation, is well worth a careful reading.*

The Crib at this age is the best centre for the little one's devotion, and should hold a prominent position throughout the year : that is one reason why it is important to have a permanent Crib in the class-room.

---

* " Dr. Montessori's Own Handbook " by Maria Montessori, London, William Heinemann, p. 75 to p. 79.

Material for short informal talks about Our Lord, Our Lady, and the Saints.

(These suggestions, if taken, should be developed).

1. St. Joseph would sometimes say, when Our Lord was a little boy at Nazareth: " Jesus, come here. I want you."
What do you think Our Lord would do? What must we do? etc.
Our Lady may have said: " Jesus, fetch me that little cup," etc.

2. Our Lord and Our Lady and St. Joseph were very poor: so sometimes they were hungry.
You see Our Lord was thinking of us, and he knew that sometimes we should be hungry too: and He wanted to feel the same as we do: so, if ever we are hungry we can say: " Jesus was hungry too," etc.

3. Our Lady used to go early every morning to fetch water. Our Lord used to go with her to carry the empty jug. Coming back again, Our Lady carried it, because it was too heavy for Our Lord.
Our Lord used always to carry something for St. Joseph when they went to work together.
Can you carry anything for Mother?

4. The Workshop. Neither Our Lady nor St. Joseph liked things left on the floor. Sometimes when St. Joseph was working,

shavings of wood (show some) would fall, and even when Our Lord was as small as you, He would pick them up and make a heap of them, and then His Mother would throw them away, so that everything might be nice and tidy.

You can do the same with bits of paper, etc., at home, and it will help Mother very much.

5. Our Lady's love of flowers.—Our Lord so often picks them for Her. We can sometimes pick daisies and buttercups and give them to Our Lady; some day we will make a daisy chain for Her.

In summer the sun was very hot where Our Lord lived, and the poor flowers died for want of water, but Our Lord used to water those He wanted for Our Lady, so as to keep them fresh, etc.

6. Our Lord played with many little boys and girls—sometimes in the fields—sometimes in the streets. He was so kind to all—so gentle—so full of love, that everyone loved Him, etc.

7. When Our Lord was small like you, He used to say His prayers, sometimes at His Mother's knee, sometimes alone. We must try and play like Him.

What do we pray for?

8. One day, when Our Lord was no longer a little Boy, but a big grown-up Man, He

D

saw a poor man, who could only use one
hand and arm—he could not move the other
at all, and it was the right hand he could
not use, so that made it all the worse, and
Our Lord was sorry for him. So He told
him to stand up so that everyone could see
him (there were a great many people there),
and Our Lord said: " Stretch out your
hand." That was just what he could not do
(show by gesture), but when Our Lord told
him, he stretched it out at once, and after
that he could use both hands and arms, just
as you can. Our Lord is always so kind when
we can't do things—He always wants to help
us.

Think how glad the poor man was!

(Any miracle of Our Lord can be told in
simple fashion, except the raising from the
dead—more suitable later—the cases of
diabolical possession, and also perhaps those
of leprosy).

9.   Many little incidents which are neither
miracles nor parables—such as Zacheus in the
sycamore tree—Our Lord in Martha's house
—Our Lord riding into Jerusalem, accompanied by the shouts of joy from the children, etc., furnish matter for conversation,
provided they are very simply dealt with.

10.   Many verses of hymns can form the
basis of a little conversation—e.g., " Jesus,
gentlest Shepherd " (a discussion on " white

sheep," " black sheep," "lost sheep," etc.),
or again :

> " As men to their gardens
> Go to seek sweet flowers,
> In our hearts, dear Jesus
> Seeks them at all hours," etc.

" Dear Angel ever at my side . . . etc.

11.   The stories and emblems of the Saints
will, if carefully chosen, furnish matter for
conversation : e.g., St. Agnes and her lamb,
St. Dorothy and her fruits and flowers, the
shamrock, etc.

OUR LORD BLESSING LITTLE CHILDREN

Tell the little ones in very simple words
how Our Lord loves us all—how when He was
on earth He loved everyone He spoke to or
who spoke to Him, but that there were some
whom He seemed to love better than others,
and among these were little children, such as
they are now.

Make the following come home, by repetition, by actions, and by pictures :—

Our Lord used to lay His Hands on the
heads of little children who came to Him or
who were carried to Him in their mothers'
arms. Our Lord used to say a prayer over
them and bless them.—(Matt. xix., 13-15).

Our Lord used to tell those who stood round, and who saw Him do this, that Heaven was full of little children like those He had just blest.

Our Lord used to put His arm round them. He took them on His knee, and their mothers used to bring them to Him, that He might just touch them with His Hand : they knew what a precious thing it would be for them if He did.

And Our Lord never refused. He loved to have His little ones near Him.—(Mark x., 13).

One day when there were many little ones round Our Lord, and the grown-up people wanted Him to send the children away that they might talk to Him instead, Our Lord called one little boy to Him and held him between His knees, turning him round to the grown-up people, that they might all see him, and He said : "Do you see this little child? He is good, obedient and gentle, and unless you are like him, you will not get into Heaven at all." Then He kissed that little boy, and sent him off to play with the others.

(See too p. 103).

(End of First Year's Course.)

SECOND YEAR'S COURSE

I. GOD THE FATHER MADE EVERYTHING

1. *God the Father made everything.* **A** picture of a loving father at home—who does so much for his children—loves them—is kind, etc. Many examples—*e.g.* their breakfast this morning—who bought it for them?

But, who made it. Go into details—Who made the milk, the flour for the bread, etc.? God—God is our Father too.

Contrast the love of our father at home with the love of our Father in Heaven. The gifts of our father on earth—our Heavenly Father's gifts. Contrast kindness, goodness, etc.

2. *What God our Father has done for us.* Once there was no light on the earth—all dark—dark—dark, and God the Father knew we should want light, and so He made a beautiful sun and hung it in the sky, to give us light. We turn away from it at night, because God our Father wants us to sleep, and we sleep better in the dark, but every morning it comes back and gives us light. God our Father made the sun. He made the evening and the morning, the stars and the moon, etc. He made our beautiful country, hills, mountains,

fields and flowers. He made the sea, rivers, snow, ice, rain, etc. He made the animals, the tiger and the lamb, etc.

3. Go through some of the other works of Creation, as simply as possible.

Get the children to suggest some and then supplement.

4. *Why did God do all this?* He did not want any of those things for Himself. He had His own beautiful Heaven, and none of these were half as beautiful as what He had there. He did not want any of them but He did want *us.*

He wanted you N—— and *you* and *you,* each of you . . . but He had to make sure that we each of us love Him, before He could have us with Him in Heaven, where He wants us to be. He will not have us there, unless we want to come. And so He made a home for us first on earth, where we could show Him that we want Him too.

This beautiful earth, with all God's gifts on it, is to be our home for a short time, until He calls us to Heaven.

He made all these things because He wants us to be happy even here.

Go over some of them again, getting children to suggest as many as possible. Dwell on the thought of God's love in each.

II. GOD OUR FATHER CAN DO EVERYTHING

1. Sometimes we ask our father at home to do something for us, and he says: "I can't."

What does he mean? That he is not able to.

God our Heavenly Father could never say, "I can't," because there is nothing good He cannot do. We know that He made everything, quite easily, out of nothing. When you ask your mother to make you a cake she cannot make it out of nothing: she needs flour and sugar and currants, and she can't make these: God did that.

2. A big strong man can carry heavy things, but he soon has to stop, and if they are very big and heavy, he cannot even move them, but God can move the mountains and even this big earth, without feeling any weight at all, more easily than you can move a feather.

There is nothing good that God cannot do, and that He will not do for each one of you if you ask Him.

Show the children some pictures of e.g. a storm at sea—the Falls of Niagara—the huge trees of the American forests—lions and tigers—anything that shows God's power strikingly, and get the thought well driven home: "God did that—He could do it a thousand times over—He made it all out of nothing."

3. *The God Who can do all things is my Friend.* A Friend Who can never say: " I can't." A Friend Who will never refuse me. A Friend Who loves me more than all my other friends put together.

If we could add all the love of our earthly father and mother, brothers, sisters, etc., till we had used up all the love there is in the whole big world, we should not have as great a heap of love as God's love for each of us. It would look such a tiny little heap beside the great mountain of God's love.

When we want to give beautiful presents to those we love, we are often stopped because we are not rich enough : that is never true of God.

We just ask Him for all we want. He listens to every word we say and then sends us what we ask for.

Is it not a happy thing to have for our best Friend, our strong God, Who can do everything ?

N.B.—In speaking to the whole class, do not suggest the idea that prayer sometimes remains unanswered. As a matter of fact, when we ask in the real spirit of Christ, and with full confidence, we can always get what we ask for : our Lord says so and the Saints verify it.

When an individual child says he has prayed for something and not got it, explain to him that perhaps his prayer had not enough faith in it—or perhaps he was asking for something selfish, and then of course he *could* not have enough faith : add, that when we ask for " temporal " things (*e.g.* fine weather), it is generally better to ask for it conditionally, on its being good for us and God's Will.

III. GOD OUR FATHER KNOWS AND SEES EVERYTHING

1. There are many things I might ask you and you would have to say, " I don't know." And there are many things you might ask me and I should have to answer, " I don't know."

You might ask me : "How is it that if a little seed is put into the ground, a beautiful flower grows up from it ?" (Show seed and flower). And I should say, " I don't know. God made the seed and the flower but I don't know how they grow."

And you might ask me, " How is it that the sheep gets wool on its back and the bird gets feathers ?" (Show pictures). I should have to say : " I don't know. I know God made the sheep and the birds like that but I don't know how He did it or how the wool and the feathers grow."

And you might ask me (make a little child and a bigger one stand for a moment side by side), "How is it that I am growing bigger every day?" And I should have to give you the same answer: "I don't know. I know all children grow bigger as they grow older and I know God makes them grow, but how He does it, I don't know."

And then you might become tired of asking me questions and of always hearing that I don't know and you might take the same questions to someone else, someone whom people said was very wise and knew a great many things, but he would give you the same answer. "My child," he would say, "I don't know." And then you might ask, "Who knows? Who can tell me?" And he would answer, "God. He knows everything. He knows how He does all these wonderful things, but He has not told us, and He alone knows."

And so there is no question that we could ask God He does not know the answer to. He knows everything and everybody and He never forgets. He knows you and me and all we are thinking of, inside our heads: all we do when we are quite alone. He loves us so much that He cannot bear to have us out of His sight, and so He is always watching to do all He can to make us happy.

If we go into the dark we cannot see, but there is no darkness for God—He sees everything—all we want—all that hurts us, etc. All we keep secret, shut away from others, God sees it all. All through our dark night He is watching us and He never forgets.

God is like a beautiful Sun always shining on us. Wherever we go the light shines into our hearts and shows God everything there.

Sometimes we have a little secret which we don't tell anybody : we keep it shut up inside our hearts quite tight. It may be a good little secret or it may not be quite so good : and we say to ourselves, " Nobody knows that—nobody but *me*." That is never true : we must say to ourselves : " Nobody knows that except God and I." He will always help us in all our secrets, if we ask Him.

It is a good thing sometimes, *e.g.* just before prayers—to have a little exercise of realising the Presence of God.

The question, reverently asked, " Who is in this room ?" each answer followed by, " Some One else," may attain the end ; or a moment's perfect silence (see p. 46); or a repetition of the words, "God is here," " God sees me," " God is loving me," etc.

IV. THE STORY OF ADAM AND EVE*

This could be dramatised up to the taking of the Apple, but not further.

* Genesis iii., 1-24.

After the description of the garden, the story falls naturally into a series of duologues : and this is the only practical dramatic form.

(a) Duologue between Adam and Eve, all joy and delight—flowers and fruit, etc., spoken of.

(b) Between Eve and the Serpent.

(c) Between Adam and Eve again, till the Voice of God is heard calling to them.

Make the children realise that the Serpent is the Devil, bent on doing great harm to both Adam and Eve.

After this, on to the end, make everything as hushed and reverent as possible. God's displeasure; Adam's fear; the attempt of Adam and Eve to excuse their sin, their failure, and then the awful punishment, pain, labour, death; the driving out from Paradise —the bitter grief of Adam and Eve.

What has happened ? *Sin.* Wrong-doing— doing what makes God displeased—what He hates.

What has happened to Adam and Eve ? Contrast between : "Before and After."

What has happened to the Earth ? Another contrast. God's work was all spoilt.

What was God going to do ? He was going to make it all right again, and in the most beautiful way possible.

He chose to send His only Son Jesus, into the world, as He was the only One who could make it all right.

He was to come, as you know, as a little Baby, and then grow up to be a man, and for love of Him God would love all men again.

But as we have just seen in Adam and Eve, pain and punishment *must* come after sin.

And as God was very much displeased at the sin of Adam and Eve He said no man, woman, or child should get to Heaven unless Jesus, His only Son, died for them.

Jesus came, He lived on earth for thirty years, and then He died in great pain on the Cross, to make that big sin all right again.

And so you and I can get to Heaven and no one can stop us. Only one thing can shut the big gates against us again, and that is our own big sin which we need never do, and please God we never shall.

But even if we did sin, though we must pray every day not to, Our Lord will make that all right too if we ask Him.

V. CALVARY THE CRUCIFIX

Early in the year show the children a Crucifix (a fairly large one).

Make them understand:

(1). That it is the same Jesus Who was born in Bethlehem—Jesus Who is God.

(2). That wicked men put Him to death, but that He let them do it because He loves each one of us so much that He died for us—to make up for sin.

(3). Answer all their questions.

(4). Teach them from the very beginning to treat the Crucifix with the greatest love and reverence.

N.B.—Do *not* tell the children that *they* put Him to death. It is not true since none of them have committed mortal sin, and it is a statement which no child can understand.

A little boy of five once asked : " Who put the nails in?" and his Mother injudiciously answered : "You, Philip, you put them in." A little later she found him on the floor with the Crucifix on his knees, having managed to detach the plaster Figure.

"Philip has taken them out," he said. "Philip never meant to put them in."

But for years after he puzzled over her words.

VI.   THE OUR FATHER

There are six points here which require careful teaching :

1. Hallowed.
2. Thy Kingdom.
3. Thy Will be done.
4. Our daily bread.
5. Trespasses and forgiveness.
6. Temptation.

Make sure that the children have definite, if incomplete, ideas about these six headings.

It is quite wrong merely to teach the words by rote and let them get into a mechanical habit of recitation.

Even if they already understand them, it is well to go over them from time to time.

1. *Hallowed*. If we said of anyone that they were strong and wise and kind and loving we should be said to *praise* them.

Who is as strong and wise, etc., as God?

Therefore we praise our good God. Just as when we hear our earthly father's name we think of him with love, so too with God.

There is another word which means praise which we keep for God's special praise—that is " hallowed."

Teach the new word in the usual way and get children to repeat:

" Our Father, who art in Heaven, hallowed be Thy Name."

2. Draw a picture of God as the King of Kings. His Kingdom, the whole earth and the whole Heavens.

How we should treat any king.

How the King of Kings.

All do not do this, therefore we pray: " Thy Kingdom come !"

God wants the little kingdom of our hearts . . . How shall we treat the King of Kings? . . . love . . . honour . . . obey.

3. *Thy Will be done.* Link on to the obedience suggested above. The children know nothing about the human will, but they understand what is meant when someone is asked, " Will you do that ?" and the answer is, " I will," or " I won't."

In the first case a promise is made to do what is asked, and so what we mean when we say " Thy Will be done " is, that God asks us to do things for Him and we answer : " Yes, I will." Also, we want everybody else to give the same answer to God. " Will you do it ?"

" Yes, I will, Lord. Thy Will be done."

4. *Our daily bread.* Bread stands for all we want in this world. All comes from our Heavenly Father . . . etc.

Allude to another Bread which they will learn more about very soon. A Bread which Our Lord alone can give them, and which is HIMSELF.

5. *Forgive us our Trespasses, etc.*

(a) When we tell Mother or Father that we are sorry and they answer : " It is all right now." That means they forgive. Apply to children's sorrow towards God and His forgiveness. It is then all right.

(b) *Trespasses.* A big word for sin, wrongdoing. Exemplify by some childish fault—temper, disobedience.

(c) "*As we forgive them that trespass against us.*"

Just as we want to be "all right" when
we have asked God's pardon, so must we
make it "all right" when our brothers or
sisters or companions say they are sorry.
We must "make it up" and forget all about
it, and we do this even if they have forgotten
to say they are sorry. If we do, then God
forgives us everything.

The story of St. Nicephorus might be told
with effect. The facts are as follows, and they
can be easily adapted to suit the capacity of
the class. They would also dramatise well.

Sapricius and Nicephorus were great friends
and loved one another like brothers, but one
day they quarrelled, and after that they would
not speak to one another. Nicephorus, realising that this was very wrong, sent three
different sets of friends to Sapricius to beg
him to forgive him. But it was no use. Then
he went himself and threw himself at the feet
of Sapricius, saying: "Forgive me!" but
Sapricius would not.

Persecution broke out against the Christians
and Sapricius confessed the Faith and was led
out to die. On the way, Nicephorus again
threw himself at his feet, saying, "O Martyr
of Christ, forgive me!"

Sapricius was again silent, but when he
reached the place of persecution, he turned
round to the executioner and said, "Strike
not, I will deny Christ."

E

Nicephorus cried to him, "O my brother, do not lose the crown so nearly won!"

But Sapricius was as obstinate in his apostasy as he had been in hatred of his brother. Perseverance was not for him but for Nicephorus, who immediately confessed he was a Christian and received the martyr's crown.

6. *Temptation.* It is a happy thing to do what God wants, and yet sometimes we feel that we should like to do something else. For instance, we see a nice box of sweets on the table and we feel that we should like to take it. It is not ours, and we know we ought not to take anything that does not belong to us. We *want* the sweets, and we do what *we* want. We know it is naughty, and if the nice box had not been on the table we should not have thought about it, but it looked so nice and so sweet, it *tempted* us—made us feel how much we should like it. We might have turned our back and walked away, that was what God wanted, but instead we did what *we* wanted and put it into our pocket and went away and ate it. Therefore we say very earnestly, "Lead us not into temptation, but deliver us from evil. Amen."

"*Evil*" means all harm, everything that hurts us. The greatest evil is sin—wrong-doing.

Explain simply the evils of poverty, of sickness, etc., but dwell a little on the fact that wrong-doing is the greatest of all evils, and that we shall be very rich and very well in Heaven, etc.

After these or similar explanations the children should say the Our Father daily, slowly and reverently, sitting, standing or kneeling, it does not matter which.

Take from time to time one or other of the petitions and talk it over with the class in a simple, homely manner so that the children may get more and more into the habit of connecting *some* thought with one or other of the words.

A habit of mere mechanical repetition is to be avoided at all costs.

When the words are quite familiar, vary this repetition by putting different pictures before the class, *e.g.*, the Crucifixion, the Crib, etc., talk a little about the picture, then say with the children the " Our Father," getting them to fix their eyes on the picture and think a little about it whilst they are saying the prayer.

It is better to divide a large class into sections for this. The rest can make daisy-chains for Our Lady, or cut out little blue or red flags to carry in a Procession, or make a paper basket to hold a few little flowers to offer to the Sacred Heart, etc., etc.

VII. THE FIRST HALF OF THE HAIL MARY

1. Recall the story of the Annunciation and how Our Lady was called " full of grace."

Obtain reasons.

Why did the Angel say, " The Lord is with thee ?"

If there is any difficulty in answering, recall Bethlehem, etc., God is always with Mary and Jesus, who is God, is with her too. Get the children to say several times, in front of Our Lady's picture, " Hail Mary, full of grace, the Lord is with Thee."

A procession to Our Lady might then be made, each child presenting one flower (a daisy will do), and repeating the words. The little flags can be carried when the flowers are not obtainable.

*2. Tell how Our Lady, when she heard the good news that Baby Jesus was coming, went to tell her cousin all about it.

Give name and awaken interest in the "Lizzies," etc., of the class. Describe the scene of the two cousins meeting. Explain St. Elizabeth's words, " You, dear Mary, are blessed more than all other women, and blessed too is your son, Jesus."

* Luke i., 39-56.

Your Mother at home is very blessed in having you as her child, but think how blessed Mary was in having Jesus, the very God, as her Son !

A recapitulation might be made by dividing the children into two bands—the Angel's band and St. Elizabeth's band.

The first band to go to Our Lady's Statue and say, " Hail, full of grace, the Lord is with thee." And St. Elizabeth's band to follow and complete the salutation.

Finally, the next day the bands could change places, so that if the words are not already known they will be learnt.

VIII.   GOD THE HOLY GHOST SPEAKS TO PEOPLE IN THEIR HEARTS

" The Holy Ghost " is not an easy lesson to give to children. You want to give them the idea of the Supreme Spirit, and yet this idea must be concreted somehow, or the children will not grasp it.

The following notes may help.

1. Compare with what our Angel Guardian

does to help us. He whispers to us to be good, keep us out of harm's way, etc.

So to the Holy Ghost whispers to our hearts, and we must listen to what He says and do it.

*2. A very simple talk about the visit which Nicodemus, a friend of Our Lord, paid Him by night.

Picture the room—the light of one little lamp, etc. Why this friend came by night— What did they talk about ?†

Heaven where Our Lord had always lived and where he had come from only a few years before.

God Who dwelt in Heaven—God the Father Who made us all—God the Son who had come on earth and was now talking to His friend. And God the Holy Ghost of Whom Nicodemus knew nothing.

So Our Lord told him that the Holy Ghost spoke to Him often in his heart and told him what to do to be good.

Our Lord said that when the Holy Ghost spoke, it was like a soft gentle wind blowing among the trees in summer time. If Nicodemus did not listen he would not hear it, but if he listened well he would hear the Holy Ghost speaking to his heart and telling him

* John iii., 1-21.

† Nelson's Bible Wall Series, " Jesus and Nicodemus," No. 224.

what to do.   And Nicodemus listened and the Holy Ghost told him not to be afraid but to be proud that he was Our Lord's friend, and Nicodemus heard, and after that he was never afraid again.

3. Another way in which this lesson could be taken would be to tell the story of Our Lord's Baptism, as we have in it a visible representation of the Blessed Trinity; but the Baptism requires much explanation, and presents so many difficulties that, on the whole, it is probably better left till later and will serve for revision of the above doctrine next year.

*4. The story of Elias very simply told.

(a) There lived once, many years ago, a holy man called Elias, who was very strong, very wise, and a great friend of God.   And there was in those days a wicked Queen called Jezabel who hated Elias, because he told her how wicked she was, and Jezabel made up her mind to kill him.

Elias was afraid, and he thought he had better run away before the wicked Queen caught him.   He ran for a long time till he was very tired and then he lay down under a big tree and fell asleep.   And God knew that he was not only tired but hungry, so He sent an Angel to him with a cake and some water, and the Angel woke Elias and told him to rise and eat.

* III Kings xix., 1-19.

Elias ate up the whole cake and drank all the water and then fell asleep again, for he was still very tired. And God let him sleep a long time and then the Angel came back with another cake and some more water and Elias awoke and ate it all, and when he had finished, the Angel told him to go to a certain mountain, which was a long way off, and that he was to live in a cave there, and that there the Holy Ghost would speak to him.

(b) Elias did just what the Angel said, and after walking a long time he came to the cave and lived there.

And one day a gentle Voice said : " What are you doing here, Elias ?" and Elias knew that the Voice was the Voice of God, and he answered humbly and reverently, telling of the wickedness of Queen Jezabel, and how he had run away from her.

And the Voice told him to go out of the cave and stand upon the mountain and there the Holy Ghost would speak to him again. And Elias went forth out of the cave and stood upon the mountain. And a great storm of wind arose, so great that all the mountain shook and some of the rocks were broken in pieces. But Elias knew that the Holy Ghost would not speak to him in a storm like this, so he stood quite still and waited, and the storm did him no harm.

It was soon over and then came a great fire,

so that all the mountain was one blaze, and it was very beautiful, though terrible, to look at. And Elias thought : " No, the Holy Ghost will not come till all is still."

(c) And then a gentle little whisper, as of a soft breeze ! Elias had on a big mantle and when he heard the gentle breeze, he buried his face in it and was afraid, because he knew that the Holy Ghost was going to speak and the Holy Ghost is God. And the Holy Ghost spoke to Elias in a soft low voice and He told him not to be afraid, for the wicked Queen would not be able to touch him, but that she herself would be punished for all her past deeds.

So Elias was comforted and he went back to his own country and worked hard for God, doing all that the Holy Ghost told him. And the wicked Queen Jezabel was punished for all her bad deeds and died miserably.

A fitting close to these lessons would be to teach the children the *Gloria Patri*.

Glory means praise, and with a little encouragement it will be easy to obtain reasons why we should praise God the Father (creation, love, etc.). God the Son (born in a stable—love, etc.). God the Holy Ghost (because He speaks to me in my heart, will never leave me, etc.). Glory be to the three Persons in one God.

Repeat the words.

There has always been glory to God, there is glory to God, there always will be glory to God.

Teach by repetition accompanied by stress on meaning, as for other prayers.

The Shamrock, used by St. Patrick to teach the doctrine of the Blessed Trinity, is a very helpful illustration.

IX. HEAVEN

1. A reference to the *Gloria Patri* and a little conversation on " World without end."

That place is called Heaven and it is the place to which we are all going. We are not going to stay here always. You have heard people talk about death. " So and so has died." It happens every day, many times a day.

What does death mean? It means that we leave this earth and go to God—and God asks : " Do you love me?" Then He looks into our heart and if He sees the answer is " Yes," He takes us in His arms, away from this world, and bears us to Heaven. And there we shall get such a grand surprise.

Get some examples of the things the children like very much—a holiday—a Christmas Tree—a day in the country—or at the seaside, etc.

Get from them, that because all these things are so nice, it is a pity that they should come to an end. Obtain that they all *do* come to an end—everything does.

2. *Speak of Heaven as a beautiful home* where we shall live for *ever*. We shall be so happy, we could not be happier, and it will *never* come to an end. When we have been there a thousand years we shall not be any nearer the end than when we first came.

Sometimes we say sadly of the holidays: " Oh, they are nearly over now !"

We shall never say that of Heaven—it will never be " nearly over." It will go on *for ever and for ever.*

3. *What is Heaven like?* We do not know : it is so beautiful, so happy, that we cannot even imagine it. Our Lord at the Last Supper was talking of Heaven to His Apostles : He had been there, so He knew what it was like ; but He was the only one Who did : He did not tell them what it was like : only that He was going to leave them and go back there.

This made them very sad, and to console them He told them that He was going to prepare a place for them in Heaven.

And He is preparing a place for us, too—to give us such a surprise : when we see our beautiful home we shall hardly be able to believe it is meant for us—but He will give it to us, and it will be our very own for *ever*.

4. *Whom shall we see in Heaven?* God—the great, beautiful God—Who loves us, and Whom we love—Our Blessed Lord—God made Man—all beauty and sweetness—so glad to welcome us, and we so glad to see Him—Our Blessed Lady, our own dear Mother Mary and St. Joseph, and so many people we have loved, whilst we were here on earth—now all so beautiful—but we shall know them all, and love them all, and have *everything* we want, everything we like and love, and we shall have it *for ever*.

(The principle: " If you want it you will have it : if you would like to do it, you will be able to :" is, of course, absolutely true, and is perhaps the best way of answering children's questions and desires concerning Heaven).

X.   THE BLESSED SACRAMENT

We were talking lately about Heaven, and how one thing we know for certain is, that we shall see Our Lord and Our Lady there : but Our Lord loved us so much that He could not bear to wait till we get to Heaven before He could have us near Him, so, when He knew that it was nearly time for Him to go to

Heaven He said to Himself: "I cannot leave them alone: I love them too much: besides what would they do without Me?"

So He did a wonderful thing—you know Our Lord is God, and He can do everything. He arranged that He would stay with us on earth, but not as He had been till then. He would come down from Heaven on our altars, whenever we wanted Him to.

Only His priests can get Him to come down like that: but they ask Him to come, every time they say *Mass*.

When you go to Church on Sunday, the Priest says Mass. It is at Mass that the priest asks Our Lord to come down, and He does so at once—always in the same wonderful way— like Bread and Wine.

It looks like Bread and Wine, but it is really Our Lord Himself.

This was a very special promise which He made when on earth, that whenever His priests ask Him, He will come immediately.

When the bell rings in the middle of Mass, it means "He is coming," and the next time it rings, it means: "He has come," and we must bow our heads and tell Him that we are glad to see Him: dear Lord Jesus, come down from Heaven, on to the altar for us.

What we must do at Mass.

1. We have a great deal to do: no time to look about or think of other things—we are

too busy. First we have to welcome Our Lord.

Exemplify by the way they greet a little friend they are glad to see. Jesus is our best Friend : so He, too, is welcome.

2. After we have told Our Lord several times that we love Him very much, we must thank Him for all the good things He has given us.

Get as many suggestions as possible.

3. The third thing we have to do is to tell Him about any little thing we have done wrong.

Suggest : going to bed without saying " good-night " to Jesus—temper—unkindness, etc.

4. And then the rest of the time we can ask for everything we want—never mind what it is.

Again get the children's suggestions and remind them to have a little talk with Our Lady, before they leave the Church.

XI. OUR LORD LIVES IN THE TABERNACLE

1. Go over the chief facts of last lesson then talk over the reasons why Our Lord does this, because He loves us and wants to stay with us.

Dwell on the fact that He does stay—day and night.

Speak, too, of the life Our Lord lives in the

Tabernacle :—waiting for us—praying for us —welcoming us—loving us.

Be careful not to encourage the idea that He is a prisoner there, or to be pitied.

Describe the Tabernacle—very beautiful— with its gold door—white silk curtains inside —the gold door locked, and Jesus within the Tabernacle, Our Lord's little golden home.

Get the children to say softly : " The Tabernacle, where Jesus is."

Talk over the great fact with them, and get them to realise some obvious results :

(a) Jesus must be often very lonely.

(b) Jesus is there always waiting for me : it is weary work to be always waiting for someone who does not come.

(c) Jesus wants me to come and visit Him. How often can I go ?

(d) It is not a kind thing to pass the door and not look in, if only for a moment.

(e) How much does Jesus love me ? Does anyone else wait for me day and night ?

(f) What shall we say to Our Lord when we go to visit Him.

Teach the children how to genuflect and give the reason. Teach them from the very beginning never to genuflect without saying a tiny prayer at the same time. Make the prayer a part of the genuflection—" Jesus, I adore Thee," or " Jesus, I love Thee," or anything else preferred, provided it be very short.

If this is taught from the beginning it will be more difficult in after life for the genuflection to become merely mechanical.

If the school is close to the church it would perhaps not be difficult to arrange that a visit be paid to the Blessed Sacrament during a part of the instruction time.   Also encourage the children to pay a tiny visit, after or before school, as they pass the church.   They soon get into the way of doing this and delight in it.

XII.   THE FLIGHT INTO EGYPT*

Link on to the visit of the Three Wise Men.

With regard to Herod it will be sufficient to say that he was a very wicked king who wanted to kill Our Lord because the Wise Men had called Our Lord King of the Jews, and Herod was jealous.

He could not find out where Our Lord was so he killed all the little babies in Bethlehem, thinking that Our Lord would be among them. It was very wicked, but the little babies were glad to die for Our Lord, and they are happy Martyrs in Heaven now.

The children can make a procession to Egypt, accompanying Our Lady and St. Joseph.

* Matt. ii., 13-18.

Show pictures of Egypt and Heliopolis. If no large ones are available show coloured postcards. (Tuck's are excellent).

Tell the story of Matariah. The following notes may help in preparation.

NOTE.—These and subsequent notes are given on the principle that we must ourselves know a great deal more on the subject than we can teach. It is hoped that they may be useful for revision when preparing the lesson.

In all the stories of the Life of Our Lord, details are a great help towards success; the same story may often, with advantage, be made to last for several consecutive days. Do not hurry, build up the pictures vividly, that they may linger in the children's minds exactly in the same way as their fairy stories do, but with a different atmosphere clinging round them.

" Where did we stop yesterday?" is a very effective way of recapitulating and reviving the keenest interest.

The stories which follow are meant to be adapted to the capacity of the particular class or set of children being taught. Children of six vary very much in this respect, and the teller of the story must judge as to how much the children can take in. *Interest* is the touchstone. Whatever interests should be dwelt on, whatever awakens no interest, should be immediately discarded.

Matariah, where tradition places the sojourn of the Holy Family in Egypt, is a few miles north of Cairo and quite near to the ancient Heliopolis. The Pyramids can be seen from there, the sand of the surrounding desert, palm trees, camels, donkeys, etc., are all much as they were, when the eyes of the Holy Family rested on them.

F

Our Lady is said to have sat with the Holy Child under a tree, before entering the village. She was very tired and thirsty. St. Joseph prayed for water and a spring sprang forth. The tree and spring are now in the enclosure of a garden which belongs to the Jesuits. The tree is a Sycamore, unlike ours, bearing the "False Fig," a fruit which the Easterns eat. The present tree is said to be a seedling from the original tree cultivated in each succeeding generation with great care.

There is a well-known picture called, "Repose in Egypt"* by Van Eyck, which represents the scene. Our Lady is seated under the tree, Our Lord is lying in her arms, St. Joseph is watching over both, and a lovely little Angel with a harp is half-kneeling, half-sitting in front of Our Lady playing for the Holy Child.

Another tradition is that Our Lady, before reaching Cairo, lodged one night in a cave which belonged to a robber and his wife. The woman was very kind to the Holy Family, and was convinced that there was something wonderful about the Holy Child.

Her own little son Dismas was covered with leprosy. She washed him in the water Our Lady had used to wash the Divine Infant, and Dismas was immediately cured.

* Published by the Perry Society.

This is Dismas, the man who grew up a robber but who died the "Good Thief."

Speak too of the tradition that the statues of the false gods in the temples fell to the ground when the Holy Family entered Heliopolis at dusk one evening, weary and footsore, and seeking shelter for the night.

XIII. NAZARETH

1. Describe Nazareth and the Holy House. These notes may help.

A cottage opening at the back into a cave in the hillside. (Recall the cave at Bethlehem).

The cottage was made of stone of a reddish pink colour, plain rough walls, one low room, to the West the only window; this part was partitioned off for Our Lady. To the East another room was also cut off, and as long as St. Joseph lived this was his room, shared by our Blessed Lord.

Often Our Lord slept on the roof, on a rug; this roof was reached from the outside by means of steps. Sometimes, in the evening, when the Holy Child was asleep on the roof, His Mother and St. Joseph would go up the steps to worship Him. The room to the East was called " the chamber without light "; we should have thought it very dark.

The central part was the room where the

Holy Family lived. It got its light from the entrance. It was almost bare of furniture—a few water-jugs, a table and a few seats made by St. Joseph, and against the rough walls some small wooden cupboards in which the earthenware vessels, used by the Holy Family, were kept. The room was very low, not more than $7\frac{1}{2}$ ft. high. There was a door in the middle of the back wall looking to the North which led straight to the cave.

(A Plan, however rough, might help the children. Compare size, etc., with school-room, and, if floor space allows, chalk outline on floor. The house was 33 ft. by 13 ft.).

Speak too of the Mary Well, still called by Her name, which tradition says Our Lord caused to spring forth for His Mother's use. It is at the extreme southern end of the village, and is now in an arched recess built by the Turks.

The women of Nazareth are famed for their beauty and the brilliancy and variety of their costumes. They still gather round the well at seven in the morning to draw water for the day.

The village, from the distance, looks like a star of white in a high mountain valley, and the scene, when the hill is climbed, and the town suddenly shows itself, is one of rare beauty. You look down into an oval hollow full of clean and bright houses.

2. Bring home to the children *why Our Lord lived like this*, by talking it over with them quietly, and answering their questions. Bring out Our Lord's love of poverty. If we want to be like Him we must be glad we are poor. His love of work—we may find later on that work is hard, but we must look at Him and do it. His love of the Cross—explain that we each have our cross to carry—that is, we must do as we are told, and sometimes what we do not like, and sometimes we have pain to bear.

Obedience. e.g., St. Joseph told Our Lord to get some wood. Our Lord went at once and showed how glad He was to go—that is what we must do.

3. *St. Joseph's work as a Carpenter.* Get from the children the kind of work a carpenter does, the things he makes and mends.

St. Joseph did all this plain, rough work, and Our Lord, Who knew all things, chose to work under St. Joseph and be taught by him. Describe St. Joseph's workshop—somewhere in the village—not attached to the cottage where he lived. Go into details—how, when Our Lord was old enough, they would set out for the workshop together early in the morning. Our Lord carrying the tools, or at any rate as many as He could manage. St. Joseph would unlock the door and they would go in. All had been left quite tidy the night before, and they would begin work at once. There would be more things to mend than to make probably, and St. Joseph would tell Our Lord what he wanted, and Our Lord would wait on him. When a piece of work was finished, Our Lord would carry it down the village street to the owner's house. He would often meet other boys who knew Him and He always had a bright smile and a kind word, so that the village folk used to speak of Mary's Son as " Sweetness." When Our Lord came to the owner's door He would humbly wait for the money to take back to St. Joseph. Sometimes the village folk were very rude and refused to pay what he asked, and Our Lord listened quietly and answered gently, and then He would go back to the workshop and give St. Joseph what He had finally got.

Make the following points clear :

1. Our Lord lived this life for *them*. He knew they would have to work hard and that people would sometimes be unkind.

2. There never was a happier home than the little house at Nazareth.*

* Nelson's Bible Wall Picture : " The Boyhood of Jesus at Nazareth," No. 5.

XIV. THE LOSS IN THE TEMPLE*

Contrast Nazareth, a little village, with Jerusalem a big city. Show some pictures of Jerusalem and of the Jews. Draw attention to the beautiful dresses and rich colouring, the beasts of burden, etc. Speak of the beautiful place where Our Lord and the Jews used to pray—not exactly a church, so it was called a Temple—there was only one in the world and it was at Jerusalem.

Explain why Our Lord did not go up to Jerusalem till He was 12 years old: He remained at Nazareth with a great friend of His Mother's who could not go either, and He, of course, did exactly what His friend told Him.

Describe the famous journey the Holy Family took, accompanied for the first time, by Our Lord: the caravans—very crowded at this time of the year—the division of men and women—the children could go with either.

Tell in story form the arrival at Jerusalem —the stay of the Holy Family there—their attitude in the Temple, etc.

Describe the Temple itself.

The following notes are given, as a help to revision, before giving the description—

* Luke ii., 41-52.

accompanied with sketches and pictures suited to the stage of development the children have reached.

Jerusalem is beautifully situated—it is a city of palaces—marble and cedar-covered—with deep valleys on three sides—and one deep cleft running south and north through the middle of the city. Standing quite alone is the Temple, the courts of which rose, terrace upon terrace, high above the city. All round were marble cloisters, cedar-roofed, and the Temple itself was a mass of snowy marble and of gold, glittering in the sunshine, with Mount Olivet as a green background.

The Holy Family would first pass the city walls—the streets were very narrow, named from the Gates to which they led and from the Bazaars, where fish, timber, wool, clothing, etc., were sold.*

The grand Palace of Herod was to the north-west of the Temple, surrounded by the Towers which the King had himself built. The space round the Temple was entirely clear of the buildings. Compare the Temple with the largest building the children know.

The Holy Family would first pass through the porches of the Temple and the cloisters, made of double rows of marble pillars. " The Royal Porch " was the most beautiful of all.

---

* Water-Street, Fish-Street, East-Street, etc.

(It was in one of these porches that Our Lord was found, by Our Lady and St. Joseph, at the end of three days).

Everybody went into the Temple by the right, and when leaving it turned to the left.

The Holy Family passed on till they reached the Eastern Gate (there were nine altogether) made of dazzling brass and covered with ornaments. It took twenty men to open and shut it, so heavy was it. It was called the Gate Beautiful, and the poor and the lame sometimes lay just outside and asked for alms.

The Holy Family then entered what was known as the Court of the Women. Here was the Treasury—thirteen boxes shaped like trumpets—into which people dropped their alms.

Then they would go up fifteen steps more to the Court of the Priests. There was a huge stone altar in the middle of this on which three fires burned. Behind it were the marble tables and everything else wanted for the Sacrifices.

Get the children to see that Our Lady and St. Joseph were making a great act of Faith, and get them to repeat their act of Faith. Tell in story form of the stay in Jerusalem and the preparations for departure, Our Lord's remaining behind and the Parents' sorrow. Answer the children's questions, and according to what they ask dwell on the facts that :

1. He was God.

2. He had to do His Father's Will.

3. It gave Our Lady great pain, but He knew we should sometimes have to give pain to those we love, so He allowed Our Lady to bear the pain to give us an example.

4. Describe the return journey and the search through Jerusalem. Make it as vivid as possible. In the early morning of the third day they pass down one of the narrow streets of Jerusalem, and in a kind of recess they see a poor cripple lying. Something in his face makes them stop, and St. Joseph bends over him and asks him if he had seen a young boy about twelve years old pass that way. The beggar's face lights up as he describes Our Lord, and Our Lady's eyes fill with tears as She listens, and her heart beats fast with hope.

"Yes," the poor cripple continues, "He passed me on His way to the Temple hard by. I shall never forget His smile nor the comfort His words brought."

They thank him and go straight to the Temple.

5. Describe the well-known picture of Hoffmann—better still, show a coloured print of it.

XV.   THE MARRIAGE FEAST OF CANA*

1.   Describe the death of St. Joseph in the arms of Jesus and Mary—how much they missed him in the house at Nazareth—how hard Our Lord worked to take his place, to console His Mother and to provide for the time when He would have to leave Her.

Tell how that day came too, when Our Lord was thirty years of age : He had told Our Lady years before that He must be busy about His Father's business, and now His Father wanted Him to go from one town to another, and preach to the people and tell them what they had to do to get to Heaven.

Some fifteen miles from Nazareth (compare with some distance the children know) there was a beautiful lake called the Lake of Galilee. All round the lake small villages and towns had been built, and it was to the chief of these Our Lord now took Our Lady.

So they closed the little house at Nazareth, where they had been so happy, and they went to Capharnaum, where Our Lady lived during Our Lord's years of teaching.

(Explain that Our Lord knew He would spend most of His time not far from the lake, and that therefore Our Lady would be nearer

* John ii., 1-12.

to Him at Capharnaum, and that He would
see more of Her).

But they were sad at leaving, and when they
got to the top of the hill behind Nazareth they
turned and looked together for the last time
at the little house they had loved so much.

2. Our Lord left Our Lady in Her new
home and began the work His Father had
given Him to do.

Talk over the following points :

Our Lord was going
> (a) To tell the people Who He was—
> the Son of God.
> (b) To do very wonderful things, to
> help them to believe Him.
> (c) To teach them what they had to
> do to get to Heaven.

At first no one believed Our Lord was God,
though He showed them He was, very plainly,
but He was so kind and good that several
people began to follow Him and to learn what
He taught them.

One day, some friends of His were going to
be married. There was to be a great feast
after the wedding, and Our Lord of course
was invited and asked to bring as many
friends as He liked.

Our Lady was there too and She had helped
in the arrangements for the feast. Our Lord

brought all those friends who had begun to follow Him, and the day was a very happy one, but towards the end of the feast Our Lady saw that the bridegroom seemed very much distressed about something.

She soon found out what it was . . . *There was no more wine* . . . There had been more people at the feast than had been expected, and the wine had run short.

Our Lady went very quietly across to where Our Blessed Lord was sitting and just whispered to Him : "They have no wine."

Our Lord seemed to hesitate a moment. He had not meant to do any *wonderful things* that day, but of course, if His Mother wanted it, He would have to. Besides He could never bear to see anyone in distress. Our Lady smiled, and as She passed the waiters on Her way back to Her place, She told them to go to Her Son and to do whatever He bade them.

3. The waiters went to Our Lord to get His orders. He pointed out six big jars that were standing against the wall and told them to fill them full of water. When they had done so, the jars were just as much as they could carry. But water is not wine, and the waiters did not understand the use of filling them with water, till Our Lord said : "Fill the empty bottles from these and pour out for the guests." And the water was immediately changed into most beautiful wine, so much better than the other

wine had been, that the bridegroom immediately asked the waiters how they had got it.

They told him, and the bridegroom at once
told all the guests. All were astonished and
cried out : "A miracle ! a miracle !"

(A miracle means something wonderful,
that only God can do.) And those who were
already Our Lord's friends and followers
began to understand for the first time that
He was God.

Make the children note that the first miracle
was worked at Our Lady's intercession.

XVI. THE RAISING OF JAIRUS'S DAUGHTER*

1. Give a picture, verbal or otherwise, of
Our Lord sitting out of doors, by the shores
of the lake, surrounded by a crowd whom He
is teaching. Try to give some idea of Eastern
colouring and costume.†

Note difference in sky, cloudless, except
when a storm is coming on. As the children
grow older, make them better and better

---

* Luke vii., 40-42; Mark v., 22-24; 35-43.

† The coloured Art Post Cards by Robert Leinweber,
called "The Holy Scripture in Pictures," five series of
the Old Testament and five of the New are excellent as
to design and colouring. They can be had from John
Crition, 34 Strada Reale, Malta.

acquainted with the shores of the Lake of
Galilee as it was in Our Lord's time. All
round the lake a grassy plain, so covered with
flowers as to be like one big garden bed.
Beyond, rich fields of corn, and in the distance, bleak bare mountain peaks.

Describe the sea-beach where Our Lord so
often sat, with His back to the lake, facing
the multitude who were seated on the grass.
Speak of the thousands of bright sails on the
clear waters—some Roman galleys (picture
needed), the fine fleet belonging to Herod, and
hundreds of fishermen's boats. The lake itself,
teeming with fish. Speak too of the trees—
the walnut tree, with which perhaps the children are familiar, the palm tree, heavily laden
with fruit (show picture), the grape, the fig,
and the olive (mark the difference with what
the children know of these in shops)—the
indigo, lotus, and the sugar-cane, the laurel-
rose, crimson in colour, often gleaming round
the lake, like a rich girdle.

Speak too of the many streams of bright
sparkling water which flow into this lake.
One called "Round Fountain," another
"Spring of the Fig Tree," another, which
feeds a large mill-wheel and then breaks into
a thousand channels and waters the thirsty
fields on its way to the lake.

To the west, the shore makes a beautiful
curve about four miles long. Here are the

towns Our Lord lived in during His teaching.
Capharnaum—the city of Jesus—was on the
north-western shore.*

Much of the above may not be suitable to
some particular class—the chief point is that
the children should have a lovely picture in
their minds of flowers and fruit, waving corn
and soft green grass in dazzling sunshine, with
restful shade from the trees and a cooling
breeze from the lake—the rich colouring
given by the dresses of the crowd—Our Lord
standing by the waters of the lake, "the most
beautiful among the Sons of Men."

2. Whilst Our Lord was one day teaching
by this lake, one of the great men of the city
arrived suddenly, evidently in great trouble.
His name was Jairus, he was a good man and
rich, and he tried to help the people with his
money. He had one little girl and only one,
whom he dearly loved. She had been very ill
for a few days—her father kept on thinking
each day she would get better but that very
morning she had died.

At first he would not believe it, but then,
seeing that it was really true, he rushed from
his house to where he knew Our Lord was
and falling at His feet, he cried out:

"Lord, my little child, my only daughter,

* Nelson's Bible Wall Pictures (" Ye are of more value
than many sparrows," No. 114), gives some idea of the
scene. Also No. 35, " Jairus's daughter."

is dying, is dead—but come, lay your hand upon her and she will live."

The crowd stood round listening. Some of his friends, however, knowing that the little girl was dead and thinking there was no hope, had run after the poor father and now arrived all out of breath.

" Do not trouble the Master—it is too late —your child is dead."

He bowed his head in sorrow, but he still believed Our Lord would help him. Our Lord looked at him and saw how deep his grief was : His own Heart grieved too and He said gently :

" Do not fear, only believe, I will save her." And He turned to go to Jairus's house followed by the crowd.

The little girl's body was lying on the bed, and the poor mother and some others were all weeping round. " She is dead," they said. " It is too late."

But with Our Lord at hand it is never " too late."

He made the crowd stay outside, and He told the father and mother that He would wake their little one from the sleep of death. Then slowly He drew near the bed and looked for a moment at the dead child. The father and mother were looking, not at her, but at Him, watching, hoping.

Our Lord, who is the Lord of Life and

G

Death, took the little hand in His and with a bright smile, said gently : "My child, arise !"

The little girl immediately opened her eyes, and in great joy jumped off the bed, full of life and health, and her father caught her in his arms. She passed from him to receive her mother's kisses. They did not know what to do for joy, nor how to thank Our Lord Who had been so good to them, and Our Lord had to remind them that it was long since the little girl had had anything to eat and that she was hungry, and then, rejoicing at the parents' joy, He went back with His followers, to the shores of the lake.

XVII. THE MIRACULOUS DRAUGHT OF FISHES*

The children will tell you that as the Lake of Galilee was full of fish, many fishermen would live on its shores.

Get them to talk about the boats, the fish, the nets, etc. Draw sketches on B.B. and show pictures. Speak of the four famous fishermen, Peter and Andrew, James and John, two sets of brothers. These four were already friends of Our Lord and followed Him at times. Their home was by the shores of the lake, in a little village north of " the City of Jesus."

* Luke v., 1-11.

Arrange the events as follows, in story form.

1. Our Lord leaves Capharnaum one evening and goes into a very quiet spot outside the town and spends the night in prayer. He tells His Apostles what He is going to do, meets some travellers, chooses the spot where He will spend the night and then kneels down.

2. The two sets of brothers at Bethsaida (name need not be given) set out in their boats for a night's fishing. All is dark, they row very hard, no fish caught, etc.

3. Morning breaks, the sun is just rising and Our Lord leaves the place where He had prayed all night and walks towards the village (Bethsaida). He meets the boats as they are returning home. The brothers do not see Him and set to work to wash their nets and boats. A glad crowd gathers round Our Lord immediately. Our Lord, however, walks straight on till He comes to Peter's boat. Peter and John are glad to see Him. He says nothing about the long night of hard work, but gets into Peter's boat and asks him to push off a little from the land.

Draw a vivid picture of this, Our Lord in the boat, Peter and Andrew with him, James and John still busy with their nets at a little distance and the crowds on the shore, in their brightly-coloured cloaks and head-dresses.

What did Our Lord, seated in Peter's boat,

tell the people that day? He told them as He had already told them, that the poor were blessed, the kind, the good, that if they wanted to be happy in Heaven, they must be obedient on earth; and they all listened and gazed at Him, as He sat in the boat, and some did as He told them and are in Heaven with Him to-day, but not all.

4. When Our Lord ceased speaking, a wonderful thing happened. He turned to St. Peter sitting in the boat by His side, and told him to row out further from the land, into deep waters beyond.

"Well, Master," St. Peter answered, "we have worked hard all night through, letting down our nets and catching nothing, but if You tell me to try again, I will." So he and St. Andrew began to row swiftly and steadily far out into the lake. They had not gone very far when Our Lord said:

"Stop!"

They laid their oars down by the side of the boat and St. Peter and St. Andrew seized the big net and let it down very quietly into the water. Immediately it began to fill with fish and such a quantity were caught that the net broke, and the two brothers were afraid of losing some of the fish.

Our Lord stood smiling at their wonder and astonishment.

On the shore they could see St. James and

St. John still cleaning their nets. It was too far for them to shout, so they began to signal, and luckily St. John saw them. He had had his eye on St. Peter's boat all the time and had wondered where Our Lord was going to when He rowed away, and now he and St. James row as fast as they can to where St. Peter and St. Andrew are struggling to keep the huge multitude of fishes in the broken net.

5. As soon as St. James and St. John got their boat close up to St. Peter's, after giving a glad look of welcome to Our Lord and receiving one in return, they set to work to empty the fish into the boat. They went on and on till they had filled St. Peter's boat, so that it would hold no more and then they fill St. James's in the same way. The two boats sink lower and lower into the water with the weight of the fish, till the fishermen feel, if they put any more in, that the boats will sink altogether, so they throw the rest of the fish (there were still many left in the net) back into the sea and draw in their broken net.

Then they stood still for a moment and gazed on the sight. Our Lord was standing quietly in St. Peter's boat, looking at them with great love, and the fish were lying, stacked in hundreds in both boats.

They knew Who it was Who had done this, Christ, the Son of God, and St. Peter, understanding it better than the others, fell on his knees at Our Lord's Feet and cried out : " Do not choose me, O Lord, to follow You, for I am a sinner."

Our Lord saw that they were frightened and He laid His Hand gently on St. Peter's shoulder : " Fear not," He said, "in future you shall catch, not fish—but men !"

Talk over these words with the children.

End by describing the last scene, when they returned to land, and leaving their boats and broken nets, " they followed Him."

The children will have much to say about this story, and about the four Apostles concerned in it.

Incidentally, tell as much as they want to know, about all four.

If there are fifty or more in the class, it will be necessary for conversational purposes, to divide into sections.

This story could, as recapitulation, take the form of duologues, etc. For instance, St. Peter and St. John, helped by St. Andrew and St. James, might tell it to a group of Our Lord's followers, who had not been present at the time and wanted to hear about it.

It is not wise to include the person of Our Lord in extempore dramatisation. It tends to spoil the imaginative idea.

Many religious stories lend themselves to

dramatisation, but the Gospels should be on a level of their own.

This objection does not, however, seem to apply to the Christmas Mysteries—the Crib represents Our Lord; and the whole is more like a Children's Service, than a school Dramatisation.

XVIII. SUFFER THE LITTLE CHILDREN TO COME UNTO ME*

Our Lord was one day on His way to Jerusalem. He had been near the lake for a long time and had worked many miracles, and had taught the people many beautiful things, and they had learnt to love Him very much. When they heard that He was going away, they were very sorry.

There were always crowds round Our Lord, and the Apostles sometimes got very tired trying to satisfy everybody.

This day they had been more than usually busy, because everybody wanted to see Our Lord to say good-bye. Many mothers had brought their children with them, for all children loved Our Lord, and He loved them,

---

* Matt. xix., 13-15; Mark x., 13-16; Luke xviii., 15-17.

and the children had cried when they heard that He was going away, and had begged to go with their mothers.*

In spite of there being so many, Our Lord said something kind to each one, and He kissed each child and put his Hand on each head, and He blessed them and sent them away happy. And they had told Him how much they loved Him, and how, even if He did go away, they would never forget Him.

This had been going on some time, and St. Peter thought, far too long. Our Lord had turned away for a moment to speak to another band of people who wanted Him, and St. Peter said to St. Andrew, his brother: "We must really put a stop to this."

They went up to some women who were waiting their turn and who had their babies in their arms.

" Go home," they said, " and take these children away, cannot you see how tired the Master is? This has been going on all the morning, and He has a long journey in front of Him. What is the use of bringing these babies to Him?"

Our Lord heard these last words and He turned sharply round.

" Not so," He said. " You are very wrong,

* Nelson's Bible Wall Pictures No. 60, " Christ blesses Little Children."

Peter, to speak thus; let all the little children come to Me, and never prevent them," and He put His arm round a little boy, who, in spite of the Apostles had crept close to Him.

"Do you not know," Our Lord went on to say : " that all little children go to Heaven, and unless you are gentle, obedient and humble like this little child, you will not go there ?"

St. Peter, and St. Andrew felt very sorry for what they had done, for Our Lord was evidently very much displeased. He loved children so much, He could not bear that anyone should keep them from Him. So He turned now to this last band and blessed them and embraced them, as He had done all the others.

In the talk with the children which follows, bring out that Our Lord is the same to-day as He was then—that He wants them near to Him now, as He did then—that very soon they will have Him closer to them, than He has yet been—He will come into their hearts, on the day of their First Communion.

XIX. MARTHA AND MARY*

1. Introduce the two sisters and their
brother Lazarus : Our Lord's great friends—
Our Lord's helpers—always ready when He
wanted something—the little house at
Bethany—close to Jerusalem—(There was
only Mount Olivet between Jerusalem and
Bethany, and so Our Lord often stayed with
Mary and Martha.) His room always ready
there—also food or rest.

2. Tell something of Jewish customs—the
feet in sandals—draw one on B.B.—result—
the feet often dirtied—needed frequent washing—use of perfumes, etc.

Speak of Magdalene after she had done very
wrong, coming to tell Our Lord about it—
tell also of the alabaster box, and the other
anointing—of Martha's faithful service—of
Magdalene's loving attention, at Our Lord's
Feet—how He loved both—but Mary most.

Talk all this over and bring out how loving
and faithful Martha and Mary were—and how
they did all they could for Our Blessed Lord
—they could not do much—still "what they
could."†

* Luke vii., 36-50; x., 38-42; John xii., 1-11; Mark
xiv., 3-9.

† Nelson's Bible Wall Pictures, "Mary and the
Alabaster Box," No. 75.

3. How did Our Lord reward this love?

(a) He forgave Magdalene all her big sins.

(b) Others often spoke unkindly of her, but He always took her part. (Give examples).

(c) Once when her brother Lazarus died Our Lord raised him to life, because He could not bear to see Mary and Martha in sorrow. (Tell the story in full if the children ask for it. St. John xi., 1-54).

(d) He let her, who had been a great sinner, stand beside His Blessed Mother at the Foot of the Cross when He was dying.

(e) And when He rose from the dead, as soon as He had seen his own dear Mother, He went straight to Magdalene to comfort her and tell Her He was still on earth.

(f) And now for ages and ages, Lazarus and Martha and Mary have been happy in Heaven, because they tried to be good to Him, when they were on earth.

Get the children to suggest that they too can help Jesus and be good to Him, e.g., by prayer, by kindness, by visits to the Blessed Sacrament, etc.

XX. THE STILLING OF THE
TEMPEST*†

Events.—1. Our Lord is in Capharnaum
and the crowds press upon Him night and
day. He cannot walk by the lake for them
and if He goes home to His Mother, they
crowd round the door. You would have
helped to do the same had you been there.

Our Lord knows that His apostles are
almost as tired as He is, and so He tells them
that they will leave the " City of Jesus " for
a time, and go across the lake to the hilly
country on the opposite side (Perea).

First He bade them disperse the crowds—
then before these had time to gather again,
they all went on board a boat—we do not
know whether it was St. Peter's or St.
James's or one of the others.

2. Our Lord made no preparation for the
journey—He was too weary, and they took
Him in the boat—just as He was. St. John
brought a pillow, etc. The apostles were very
quiet and silent, anxious not to wake Him.

3. Several other boats had started with
theirs, for it was a lovely evening and the

* Nelson's Bible Wall Pictures: " Jesus Stilling the
Storm," No. 34.

† Matt. vii., 13-23; Mark iv., 35-40; Luke vii., 22-26.

dark sky was lit with stars, but scarcely had
our Lord's eyes closed in sleep than everything changed. Explain with what sudden-
ness most violent storms sometimes burst on
the sea of Galilee. The icy cold wind from the
north blows down upon the lake and makes
the sea rage with anger. The huge waves play
with the fishermen's boats as if they were
walnut-shells—the sails are torn away, the
masts are broken, and the waters beat in on
every side. (Show pictures of storms at sea).

This time the boats that had started with
Our Lord were all scattered in different direc-
tions. The apostles rowed desperately against
the wind; they did not dare to wake Our
Lord, and they wondered how He could still
sleep, for the wind was roaring, and the boat
was being tossed high and low.

It was only when they felt that it was
actually sinking beneath their feet that they
threw themselves upon Our Lord, calling upon
Him loudly and in agony:

"Master, save us, we perish!"

Our Lord rose very quietly and He seemed
more anxious to calm their fears than to still
the raging sea. "Why are you afraid?" He
asked. And as the Apostles heard His gentle
Voice, they felt ashamed that they had ever
been afraid when He was near.

Then He turned His face towards the sea—
He spoke to the winds and the waves—"Be

quiet," He said, " peace, be still!'" And He had hardly said the words when the waters became quite calm and the wind ceased and all was perfectly still—for the winds and the sea obey God and only God. The clouds were gone, the stars shone out, and without any more rowing, the boat gently touched the shore on the opposite side to Capharnaum.

The Apostles were quite silent too. They understood how foolish it is to be afraid when Our Lord is there.

There were some sailors too in the boat, who had been quite sure they were going to be drowned, and they too were full of gratitude and astonishment. " Who is this?" they asked. " This is no ordinary man. He commands the winds and the waves and they obey Him!"

XXI. CALVARY

1. Talk over the following points with the children :

(a) Our Blessed Lord, Who is God, loves them very much. When we love people very much, we want to have them near us.

Our Blessed Lord always wanted and still wants to have each one of us near Him in Heaven.

(b) But His Heavenly Father was displeased with all men because man had sinned, and He would not have us in Heaven till that sin had been made all right.

(c) Our Lord knew that He alone could make that sin all right, and that is why He came down from Heaven.

(d) Now, He might have done this in many ways: *e.g.*, He might have come on earth, as a great King.

How did He come?

Or at any rate, He might have lived a very easy life on earth.

Was it very easy?

You will wonder why He was born so poor and why He lived so hard a life. Because He thought to Himself: "All the men and women and children I am going to save will not be rich. They will not have easy lives. They will not be able to have everything they like, so I will not either. I want to have them in Heaven with Me, and so I want to show them how to get there. And if they are to get to Heaven they must be poor. They must work hard, and they must do the things they don't like. So I will choose for Myself a hard life. If I do that first they will follow Me."

(e) And the chief thing Our Lord wanted to teach us, is that He loves us—"I must make quite sure they learn of that."

And so He made up His mind, that He would die for us. He knew that if He died for us, we could not doubt His love.

There were wicked people on earth, in those days, as there are wicked people now—and He let those wicked people take hold of Him and they hated Him, as wicked people do now —and they killed Him, by nailing Him to a Cross, with four big nails, one through each Hand, and one through each Foot. And He hung on that Cross for you and for me, for three hours in terrible pain and then He died. (Picture explained.)

And all our sin was forgiven, and Our Heavenly Father took us all as His Children for Jesus's sake—and the two beautiful gates of Heaven were flung open wide, so that we might get in—for they had been locked till then—and Our Lord, Who only remained dead three days, raised Himself from the dead, all beautiful and bright, and He went up to Heaven, forty days after, and is waiting there now, till our life here is finished, and we have shown Him that we love Him, and then He will come and take us to Heaven too, because He bought Heaven for us, the day He died.

This should be followed by several other lessons, in which the children's questions are answered—pictures are shown and the story of Calvary told, though not in detail.*

In all of these, dwell on the great truth, "He died *for me*, and He loves *me*."

XXII.   EASTER DAY†‡

This lesson will be best as a story.

It should bring out that Our Lord is God— He died because He chose to—and He took up His life again just when He chose—only God could do this.

The story could be divided into the following scenes.

1.   The Earthquake—the Angel rolling back a very heavy stone, which had closed up the cave where Our Lord's Body had been laid; the face of the Angel like lightning— dress, like dazzling snow.

2.   The tomb empty, because Our Lord had Himself lifted up His Body and made it full of life—bright and beautiful—as it had never been before, and then He had left the tomb and gone to console His holy Mother.

3.   All is quiet again and some of Our Lord's

* Nelson's Bible Wall Pictures: "Christ Crucified," No. 84.

† Nelson's Bible Wall Pictures: "Christ risen from the dead." No. 137.

‡ Matt. xxviii., 1-15; Mark xvi., 1-11; John xxi., 1-18.

H

friends—St. Mary Magdalene, St. Martha and others are seen coming up towards the Tomb. Speak of the ointment they carry—the Angel sitting at the right hand of the dark cave— His words—"Do not be afraid—I know Whom you are looking for—Jesus of Nazareth —He is risen—Go and tell the good news to Peter and the others—you will soon see the Lord, risen from the dead."

4. They turned away in great joy, though still in fear—but Magdalene, who loved Him best stayed behind—She could not feel any joy till she had seen Him again.

She looked into the tomb to make quite sure that Our Lord's Body was not there. Through her tears she saw two Angels seated inside, and she told them that someone had taken Our Lord away, and she did not know where He was.

And then she saw Someone else standing close by, but because she was crying so bitterly she did not see Who it was.

Someone said: "Why are you crying? What do you want?"

She did not look up, but thought He was the gardener . . .

Then Our Lord Himself, for it was He, called her by her name: "Mary!" and with a great cry of joy, she fell at His Feet, saying: "Master! dear Master!"

And after Our Lord had comforted her He

told her that He was going to stay a little longer on earth before going back to Heaven, and that she was to go to all His friends and tell them the glad news, and that that very day they were to see Him.

The road to Emmaus*; the Apparition to the Apostles on Easter Sunday evening† : the Lake of Tiberias and St. Peter's three-fold act of love,‡ are the three Apparitions which will appeal most to the children.

Each story should bring out Our Lord's love, and that :

1. Neither the hate shewn by His enemies, nor all the bitter pain, nor the being left alone by His friends to die, had made Him love them less.

2. His one thought now was to console and comfort them.

3. He stayed for forty days, because He could not bear to leave them till they were happy, and really believed He was the same Lord they had known before, and also because He had so much to teach them still.

* Luke xxiv., 13-44.

† John xx., 24-31.

‡ John xxi., 1-24.

XXIII. The ASCENSION*

A picture here is essential, as without it the words will not give any idea.

Having got the children to examine the picture carefully get them to question you about it.

Talk over points like the following :

> Where is Our Lord going to ?
> Why is He going ?
> For how long ?
> Is anyone going with Him ?
> Whom will He see when He gets to Heaven ?
> Who said good-bye to Him ?
> Why were those, who were left behind, both glad and sorry ?
> Why did His Mother not go too ? etc.

(End of Second Year's Course.)

* Mark xvi., 19-20; Luke xxiv., 50-63.

THIRD YEAR'S COURSE.

1. FAITH, HOPE AND CHARITY

1. Get the children to understand, by homely examples, the meaning of the three theological virtues, *e.g.*, a child, who is fond of joking, rushes into the room excitedly to tell them that a big tree has been blown down. They run off to *see*, they find it is so and then they believe. This is not Faith.

Their father tells them that when he was in town yesterday, there was a bad motor accident. They are immediately sure there was; they did not see it, they had heard nothing about it from anybody else, but father said so—that is quite enough, etc.

2. In the same kind of way teach, with regard to Hope, that it includes belief in someone's knowledge, goodness and power, *e.g.*, they hope for a present from someone who knows them, who loves them and has the power to give it them. Apply this to God, to Heaven and to all God's gifts.

3. What love means : (a) choice—preference; (b) willingness to give.

(a) There must be some reason for the choice. We love the people who love us and are kind to us, therefore we love God. We choose God as our friend—our chief love, therefore we give God things, which we think He would like. (b) Get the children to suggest examples—enforce idea of self-denial—giving up to God, because we love Him, etc.

Some simple examples might be given of how these things make sunshine in our hearts. Wrong-doing brings a cloud, and then we cannot see the sun, but if we tell Our Lord we are sorry, then the cloud melts away and the sunshine comes back. With regard to the Acts of Faith, Hope and Charity by far the best are those the children make for themselves, and they should be encouraged to do this as often and in as many different ways as possible.

Suggested Acts that might be learnt by heart.

Faith. My God, I believe every word which You have said, because You are God and cannot make a mistake.

Hope. My God, I hope You will give me all I need now and till I come to die, and then that You will let me see You and be with You in Heaven.

Love. My God, I love You with my whole heart because You are so good, so beautiful and so kind to me.

Sorrow. O Jesus, my God, I love You because You are so good, I am very sorry that I have sinned against You, and I will not sin any more.

II. THE BLESSED TRINITY

1. By conversation revise the children's knowledge of each of the Divine Persons. Guide their questions on to the following or similar lines:

Show the children some flowers; let them admire them, then ask: "Where were these flowers six months ago?" "Nowhere."

"And you: how old are you?" "Six." "Where were you seven years ago?" "Nowhere."

"And mother? She was once a little girl, and a few years before that where was she? And grandmother?" etc.

There was a time when everything on this earth was *nowhere*. But God? There never was a time when **He** was *nowhere*. He was always there, etc.

That which can never die is called a spirit. Our soul is a little spirit and so can never die. God is the Great Spirit Who has always lived, lives and will always live.

Our soul lives and will always live in Heaven, with God, if we are good—for God the Father is the good Father of each one of us—and He wants His children to live at home with Him.

2. Revise the children's knowledge of Our Lord's Life. Reimpress the fact that He is

God—God the Son—equal to the Father, as beautiful, as powerful, as good.

God the Father sent His Son into the world to die for us, and show us how to get to Heaven.

3. Remind the children how St. Peter and the other Apostles were chosen by Our Lord to work with Him, whilst He was upon earth. After the Ascension what were the Apostles to do? Which of them was to fill Our Lord's place? Whose boat did Our Lord teach from? etc.

Recall the story of the Apparition by the Lake of Tiberias. To whom did Our Lord say, "Feed My Lambs."

So Our Lord had chosen St. Peter to take His place. St. Peter was therefore at the head of all the Apostles, and of all those who believed in Our Lord. St. Peter was Pope, he was the first, and since his time there has always been a Pope. When St. Peter died another was chosen. (If children ask his name, give it—St. Linus.) Give name of present Pope, with some details of where he lives, what he does, etc.

The Pope tells us what to believe and what to do, he cannot make a mistake about this— Why not? Because the Holy Ghost tells the Pope what to teach, and what to tell us to do, and the Holy Ghost is God, and God can never make a mistake.

Before Our Lord went up to Heaven, He promised St. Peter this, that He would send the Holy Ghost from Heaven, Who would stay here on earth and tell the Pope, and the Priests and everybody what they were to do.

If He is on earth why cannot we see Him?

Because the Holy Ghost is God . . . the Great Spirit.

Refer to their own souls, which they cannot see, and recall the stories of Nicodemus, Elias, etc.

The air is a fairly good example of a thing which the children know exists, but which they " cannot see."

Insist on the fact that the three divine Persons are one God. End by the story of the coming of the Holy Ghost on Whitsunday.

III. THE APOSTLES' CREED

The Creed should be learnt by heart. Make the children understand that it is a beautiful act of Faith, in which we remind God of some of the chief things we know about Him, about His Son Our Lord Jesus Christ, and of all He did for us, and about the Holy Ghost and of all He does. Get children to learn one of these divisions at a time.

In connection with the Creed, a little dramatisation might be helpful.

Scene : Rome in the second century.

Scene I. Some pagan converts, being received into the Church. Before Baptism they have to repeat the Apostles' Creed.

Scene II. The trial or martyrdom of these same converts, who answer the judge's questions by repeating the Creed.

IV. CONFESSION. (A story leading up to it)

Introduction. When Our Lord was on earth, He was always trying to get people to believe that He loved them. He worked very hard for this ; He was forever doing kind things : making sick people well again, curing their eyes or their ears, or whatever it was that was wrong with them, and saying loving, kind words to comfort them when they were crying. The people seem often to have been very stupid and not to have understood that He did all this *because* He loved them. You and I must not be stupid but know that He loves us, and likes us, and wants us to be near Him always.

Some of these people thought that they themselves were very good, which is a silly

thing to do, and they used to point out other
people and say they were not good at all, and
then they pointed back at themselves and
said : " Just look at the difference." that was
unkind, and no unkind person can be good,
it was also untrue. (Tell the story of the
Pharisee and the Publican, *very* simply—and
apply to children.)*

Now Our Lord loved these poor people,
who were treated so unkindly, very much,
even though it was quite true that they had
done wrong. And very often He made them
His special friends, and He got them to understand that when we have done wrong, He just
loves us to run to Him and to say so and to
tell Him how sorry we are and that we won't
do it again. And then He makes it quite all
right again and we are greater friends with
Him than before.

One day, when Our Lord was talking to
some poor sinners, they asked Him to tell
them a story—they were as fond of stories as
you are—and Our Lord told them this " truly-
true " story, which I am going to tell you.†

" There was once a certain man, whom I
knew very well, who had two sons; the
younger knew that his father was rich and
that he too would be rich when his father died,
but he thought that would not be for a long

* Luke xviii., 9-14.
† Luke xv., 11-24.

time, and he did not like to think of his
father dying, so he said : ' Give me now my
share of everything.'

"And his kind father gave him, then and
there, his whole share.

" Then the younger son went off, far, far
away, where his father could not even get
news of him and he wasted *all* his money.

"And when he had not a penny left, he
turned to his companions who had helped him
to spend it all and asked them for some.

"But they said : ' No, it is all your own
fault. We have no money for you.'

" The younger son did not know what to do,
for everything was so dear in that country just
then—the weather had been very bad—there
was no harvest and everyone was starving.

" Then he grew very miserable and he
thought of his happy home and his kind father
and how all the servants there were well-fed
and taken care of, and how much dearer he
was to his father than they could be. And so
he made up his mind.

" ' I will go to my father and I will say :
" Father, I have done very wrong towards
God and towards you. I don't deserve to be
called your child any longer. Let me be one
of your servants and I will serve you and
never do wrong again." '

" He started for home immediately, and
what was his joy, when, as he was still a long

way off, he saw his father standing at the top of the hill he was climbing, with his arms stretched out towards him.

" He had been waiting and watching for him all the time. And the poor boy rushed into his arms, sobbing and saying: ' Father, I have done very wrong: I don't deserve to be called your son.' He could not get any further. His father would not let him finish, but fell on his neck and kissed him. And they went home together—the father trembling with joy—the son still sobbing, but so happy because he had told his father everything, and he knew he was forgiven.*

"As soon as they got home, his father told the servants to bring some beautiful clothes for his son to wear and to put a ring on his finger showing that he was his son again, and to make a big feast, because he said : ' Let us eat and be merry, for my son was dead and has come to life again—he was lost and is found.' "

When the children are talking this story over with you, dwell on the *joy* of confession and forgiveness.

The younger son had *made it all right again.*

* Nelson's Bible Wall Pictures: " The Prodigal Son," No. 57.

He felt *happy inside*—he got back all he had lost.

He went to confession to his father, and that is what we have to do to Our Lord.

When we have done wrong we have to go to Our Lord and to say so.

" Jesus, I have done wrong and I am very sorry. I have been disobedient," or " I have been unkind," or " I lost my temper and fought with my companions," or " I was rude and answered back," or *whatever it is* that we have done, which we think was wrong. Of course, people who tell lies or steal must be sure to tell the priest about it, but if we say our prayers well, there is no reason why we should ever do such things.

If we have fought with our little brother or sister, we should say so, but we must not give the name of the person we fought with. We are only busy about our *own* sins.

The priest is there in Our Lord's place and when we tell the priest, it is the same as if we told Our Lord.

The younger son was very sorry and promised never to do these wrong things again, and that is what we must do too.

We *are* very sorry:

1. Because God is so good to us and we have not been good to Him.

2. Because God hates sin—wrong-doing, and we have done what God hates.

3. Because Our Blessed Lord died for us, and instead of doing all we could for Him, we have done what He does not want us to do.

4. Because Our Lord is sorry and Our Lady is sorry and so too our Guardian Angel, and so we tell each of them in turn not to be sorry any more, because we are going to be good and not do wrong again.

Do not tell the children that there is nothing to be frightened about, as that will probably give them some idea of fear which they need not have.

End the lesson by the act of contrition, given above, or by some equivalent one.

V. GOING TO CONFESSION

This is a very simple thing.

1. We ask the priest to bless us : " Please Father, bless me."

2. We tell our sins to the priest, which is the same thing as telling them to Our Lord. Our Lord forgets all about them as soon as He has forgiven us, and so does the priest.

3. Then the priest talks to us for a little time and we must listen to what he says and do whatever he tells us to do. He will tell us to say some prayer we know very well—per-

haps the Our Father or some Hail Maries. This is called the Penance.

Explain by reference to some everyday example of punishment (penance) *e.g.* "sent to bed early," or not allowed to go out to play, etc.

The Penance which the priest bids us say is the little punishment which Our Lord gives us for having done wrong. It is very small, but we must listen attentively when the priest tells us what it is to be, and we must be sure to say it afterwards.

Recapitulate under three simple headings :
  Telling our sins.
  Listening to what the priest says.
  Remembering what prayer he has told us to say.

4. And then a wonderful thing happens.

The priest will ask you to tell Our Lord again that you are very sorry for having done wrong, and you repeat several times very softly : " Jesus, I am very sorry. I love You. I will not do it again."

And whilst you are saying this the priest will say some words over you, which you will not understand. They are wonderful words, some of the most wonderful words the priest ever says, and whilst he is saying them Our Blessed Lord is pouring His Precious Blood over your soul, so that when you come away

from Confession your soul is as white as snow
and dazzling with the beautiful red jewels of
His Precious Blood.

You may be quite happy then—all that was
wrong has been made quite right and the
priest will say : " God bless you," and you go
away, feeling so good and so happy, and Our
Lord loves you more than He ever did before.

The Confessional is rather a frightening
place to a six-year-old child, especially if it
is dark—and it is essential to keep away every
idea of fear.

Take the band who are preparing for " First
Confession " to the Church some day, when
nothing is going on, and make them go into
the Confessional and examine it in all its details, so as to prevent their feeling the place
strange when the time comes for Confession.

VI.   THANKSGIVING AFTER CONFESSION

Whenever we get a present we must thank
for it—in Confession we receive a beautiful
present, so when the priest sends us away, we
go back to our place in the church and thank
our dear Lord for having made it all right, for
having poured His Precious Blood on our soul,

I

and for making us good, so that it will be easier not to do wrong again.

Then we say our Penance because the priest told us to, and because it is our little punishment—so we say it slowly and carefully. Then we turn to Our Lord again and ask Him again to help us never to do the wrong thing, whatever it was, we have told the priest about,— we can talk to Him as long as we like—and we ask Our Lady to help us because She is our Mother, and all mothers like to have good children, and we ask our Guardian Angel to look after our promise and not let us forget it. We might also say the prayer, " Heart of Jesus, look on me "* : and we ask Our Lord to give us His blessing before we go away.

Recapitulate the big points, varying with different stories, until the children are quite at home with what they have to do, and with what it all means.

It is not wise to let the children *play* at "going to Confession." If they are well prepared the first time, they will need but little help for subsequent Confessions, but without using any compulsion or introducing routine, which is fatal to right practice after they leave school, try to obtain regular fortnightly Con-

* "A Child's Prayers to Jesus," by Father W. Roche, S.J. Longmans, Green & Co.   Price 1/-

fession from the first. Early habits are not easily eradicated. And from time to time, take a suitable miracle or parable (the cleansing of the leper, St. Mary Magdalene, the Good Thief, the Lost Sheep, etc.) and talk it over, in connection with Confession. The important point is, of course, sorrow and purpose of amendment, not so much the examination of conscience.

VII. THE FEEDING OF THE FIVE THOUSAND*

Our Lord had one day been preaching to a great crowd of people not far from the lake. It was now evening and the sun had all but set. The crowd was still staying on, and some of the Apostles thought it was high time Our Lord sent them home.

Our Lord was at that moment talking to one of His friends, whom He dearly loved, called Philip. " Philip," He said, " all these men and women are hungry. Where can we get bread for them ?"

St. Philip answered, " Lord, even if we could find a shop near at hand, it would cost more than 200 pence to feed all these, and we

* Matt. xv., 32-39; Mark vi., 35-45; John vi., 1-15.

are very poor. There are 5,000 men and women, and there are the children besides."

Our Lord did not like to think of the children, especially, being hungry.

Just at that moment, up came St. Peter and St. John and some of the others. " Lord," they said, " There is nothing to eat here : it is nearly sunset : send away all these people and let them go into the nearest towns and buy some bread for themselves."

But our Lord answered, " There is no need for them to go : you give them something to eat."

They looked at one another astonished and St. Philip repeated, " Lord, I told You, if You can give us 200 pence we might be able to get bread enough."

Our Lord looked rather sad for a moment, because the Apostles did not trust Him enough, but He only answered, " How many loaves have you got ?"

St. Andrew said, " There is a boy here with a basket : he has five loaves and two little fishes—but that is no good."

Our Lord said, " Bring the loaves to Me." And they brought them.

" Make all the people sit down on the grass in groups of hundreds and fifties."

The Apostles did this, and our Lord raised His Eyes and looked at the crowd.

There were about sixty big groups in all and

they filled a large space, so that some seemed
quite far away, and in their bright-coloured
dresses they looked like so many flower-beds in
the long grass. Our Lord blessed the loaves
and then broke them into twelve pieces, and
said : " Go now and feed the 5,000 with that."

It was very wonderful to watch.   The
Apostles began breaking off large pieces of
bread, one after another, from the half-loaf
they had in their hands and the bread never
grew less but there was always more and
more, and each Apostle fed over 400 people
from this little half-loaf, and they all had
enough and more than enough.

Then our Lord blessed the little fishes—
there were only two remember—and sent His
Apostles round with them, and the fish multi-
plied, so that instead of two, there were
thousands of fish, and when all the 5,000 had
been served, the Apostles came and stood by
our Lord in silence.

They had a great deal to think about—He
was always giving them these glorious sur-
prises—always showing more power and more
love, and they saw and they knew that He
must be God, and they prayed to trust Him
always.

And when the meal was over, Our Lord told
His Apostles each to take a basket and collect
all the pieces of bread and fish that were lying
about (He did not like anything to be wasted).

And the Apostles filled twelve baskets of what was over, though the bread and fish to begin with would not have filled one.

Then the crowd rose in great excitement and joy—they too, declared that Our Lord was God, but our Lord stopped their shouting and sent them away quietly to their homes.

VIII. THE TRIUMPHAL ENTRY INTO JERUSALEM*

This story lends itself easily to dramatisation : the children can form a procession, carrying little branches if easily obtainable. (A little twig with a leaf is enough, or some grass).

The door of the schoolroom can represent the door of the Church, as on Palm Sunday, when the procession takes place.

Do not bring in any representative of Our Lord Himself—there is none in the Palm Sunday Procession.

Tell the story first, of course, and bring out the idea that they are going to sing in honour of Our Lord—they would not like the Jews to honour Him more than they.

Divide the children into two choirs, one inside, the other outside the door—the knock-

* Matt. xxi., 1-12.

ing, etc., is dramatic. (See Missal for Palm Sunday: also Education Series—T. Shields, Education Press, Washington, but obtainable from any Catholic Bookseller. Religion Book III., p. 108.)

The children might sing the two easiest verses of the " Hymn for Palm Sunday." A picture will help.*

IX.   THE LAST SUPPER

Leaving out the meaning of Pasch and the Sacrifice of the Paschal Lamb, describe as the

First Scene.† Our Lord telling St. Peter and St. John to go into the city and prepare their supper for them, one Thursday evening. It was to be a very solemn supper, for He knew that He was to die the next day, and it was the last time before His death, He was to see all His Apostles together.

Bring in about the man carrying the jug of water, the large dining-room, etc.

Second Scene.‡ Show an oleograph of Leonardo da Vinci's Last Supper. Get the children to describe it and to notice the faces of the Apostles.

* Nelson's Bible Wall Series : " The Triumphal Entry."

† Mark xiv., 12-16.

‡ John xiii., 1-15; Matt. xxvi., 26-30; Luke xxii., 14-20.

Leave out about Judas unless the children have already had his full story—it is a most effective one, but should stand out alone, and may well be left till next year.

Dwell on some of the loving words of Our Lord—His desire to eat this Supper with them before He suffered—His love—how He loved them *to the end.*

Third Scene. The Institution of the Blessed Sacrament.

Our Lord was going to show His Love in a wonderful way—so wonderful that if He had not told us, we could never have imagined it.

He was going to die the very next day— He knew how lonely all who loved Him would be, and, as God, He could see on through all the time to come—He saw you and me—each one of us—and He knew how badly we should need Him for a Friend—so He did the most wonderful thing—He took bread into His holy Hands, blessed it, and it was immediately changed into His own Body and Blood, and He gave It to His Apostles and said : " Take and eat—This is My Body." And the wine too He changed into His Blood, and He told the Apostles to do what He had done, and because again, He thought of you and me as well as of the Apostles, He has told all His priests to do the same thing—so that in the Holy Mass, when the priest says the same words as Our Blessed Lord said, the bread and wine on the altar are changed into His Body and Blood.

Teach *very slowly*, dwelling on each action.

Our Lord Himself is there, true God and Man, the same Lord, Who was born for us, at Bethlehem, etc.

And when you make your First Communion, Our Lord will come into your hearts, under the form of bread, just as He came into the hearts of the Apostles, that Thursday night.

X. THE REAL PRESENCE

1. Recall all the children know about Our Lord's life in the Tabernacle—how He loves us to visit Him there—get suggestions as to how the time of such visits should be spent.

Refer to the fact that Our Lord is there, by night as by day.

Why? In case someone wants Him—the monks and nuns who pray by night, as well as by day—the sick, etc.

2. Explain the Service of Benediction.

The lights and flowers are there as gifts to Our Lord, and to help us to think of Him.

We may look at Our Lord on His golden Throne all the time, because He is there expressly that we may see Him, and He is doing for us, who are kneeling round Him, just what He did for the crowds who pressed round Him by the lake.

He loves, He cures, He teaches, He blesses us from His throne. Speak of the big blessing at the end.

3. The account of St. Tarcisius, patron of First Communicants, might be given in story form and his martyrdom in full. (See "Fabiola" by Cardinal Wiseman: Chapter XXII. The Viaticum.)

XI. THE HOLY MASS*

1. Talk over going to church on Sunday.

Why we go? Not merely to say our prayers —we go because we want to be present when something very wonderful is going on. What is that?

It is called the Holy Mass, and it is the most wonderful thing that ever takes place on earth.

What do we see?

Perhaps we cannot see very much from our place, but we see the priest at the altar (B.B. sketch or picture of the altar) (See many pictures in the Children's Bread: Pt. 1, by Father Roche, S.J.)

* "The Little Ones' Mass Book," with its helpful pictures and simple prayers, is as good a prayer book for little children as one could wish for. Published by Messrs. Sands & Co., 15 King Street, Covent Garden, London, and Edinburgh and Glasgow. Price 3d.

The priest is not merely praying. He is doing this wonderful thing, the same thing Our Lord did at the Last Supper. You remember how Our Lord then took bread and wine and blessed them. What did they become?

And you remember too how He has told everyone of His priests to do what He had done, and He has made it easy for them to do it. That is what is going on during Mass.

Recapitulate slowly and impressively, and answer children's questions.

1. The priest does what Our Lord did at the Last Supper.

2. The bread and wine are changed into Our Lord, the same Lord as at Bethlehem. . . (Expand this.)

3. He is there, alive, beautiful, glorious, able to do whatever He likes, and above all, loving each one of them.

XII. HOLY COMMUNION

1. Get the children's answers to the question: "What has Our Lord done for me?" Suggest and supplement.

2. His greatest gift has yet to come, He is going to give Himself to me, wholly and entirely in Holy Communion. He thought that even the Holy Mass did not bring Him close

enough. He wants to come into my very heart. This is what Holy Communion means, Our Lord Himself, under the form of a little piece of white bread, enters our hearts and makes them His own.

Recall what the children have already learnt about the consecration. Our Lord Himself is then on the altar, but we are kneeling in the Church, and when we love a person very dearly, we do not like to see them far away.

If they saw their mother standing at the top of the stairs and they were at the bottom they would run up the stairs to meet her and she would take them in her arms. That is what Our Lord does. He calls each one of us from the altar, "Come, I want *you*. I want to be closer to you than father or mother can be, because I am your God, so come up the altar steps and the priest will give Me to you."

And then with great faith and hope and love, we do what Our Lord tells us. We get up very quietly from our place, we keep our eyes down and our hands joined and we go and kneel in front of the altar, and the priest comes down from the altar, holding what looks like a little white circle of bread, but we know better; we know that it is our Lord Himself, because He has said so, and the priest places the little white circle of bread on our tongue, we swallow it, and we receive Our Lord into our hearts, and He is our very own.

And then we go back to our place, bearing our treasure very carefully and we listen to what Our Lord says to us in our hearts and we answer and talk to Him.

Enlarge a little on the wonderful moments which follow.

XIII.   THE EFFECTS OF HOLY COMMUNION

1.   Use the ordinary example of food for the body and food for the soul, therefore strength against temptation.

2.   Our Lord makes us holy, nothing makes us so holy as Holy Communion. We get holier every time we receive Our Lord, and all the time He is in our hearts He is working hard at making us more like Himself.

3.   He forgives all small faults and wrong-doing.

4.   When we die, our bodies are put into the earth and they crumble to dust, but if we have received Our Lord in Holy Communion, He will raise them up again and make them beautiful and glorious in Heaven.

With the help of the children's pennies, get them each to make a little prayer-book. A few small sheets of brown paper stitched together make a booklet. The child pastes his own pictures in, bought with his pennies, and added to from collections of pious pictures and postcards and also advertisements, cut out of catalogues. Write a title for him, "My Prayer-book " and paste it on to the cover. His having helped to make it doubles the charm.

The children could write out one or two of "The Child's Prayers to Jesus," by Father Roche, in their own prayer-book, e.g., "Most Sweet Jesus in Heaven," or any other preferred, for thanksgiving, etc.

N.B.—The prayer-book a child uses on his first communion day should be the one he uses all through the time of preparation—*not* a new one—a clean white paper cover will brighten it up.

XIV. REMOTE PREPARATION FOR FIRST COMMUNION

It is very advantageous during the few weeks that precede the First Communion to keep the thought of it constantly before the children during the day, and the only way to do this is to give them something to do which will, as it were, keep them busy.

A few examples will make the meaning clear.

1. They might make up their mind to prepare a room for Our Lord, and determine

how it shall be furnished. It must be clean, therefore I must not be naughty as that would stain it. It must have a nice carpet, *e.g.*, I will not cry when I hurt myself. The walls must have pictures; each time I think of a scene in Our Lord's Life, that is putting a picture on the wall, and when He sees it, it will feel just like home for Him.

I must have a little lamp like the one He has in the church, and it must burn brightly, therefore acts of kindness, etc.

2. I must prepare a garden for Him—pull up the weeds—plant the flowers, *e.g.*, Forget-Me-nots (thoughts of Him), red flowers (thoughts of His Passion), etc., etc.

3. I must give Him a Crown of Flowers instead of that cruel Crown of Thorns. I will do without things I like, etc.

4. I must make some clothes for the little Infant Jesus. (The stitches to be made by acts of love, etc.).

5. I must make a little crib for Jesus to lie in. Some acts made gather the straw, others to make the manger, etc., the children can be the sheep, and draw nearer and nearer as the time goes on; little pictures of sheep, made to stand, representing them at the crib, etc., are helpful.

6. I will furnish a big dining-room, like the one for the Last Supper, etc.

A certain amount of latitude should be given

as to what each child may choose to do— their suggestions should be taken first, and the above or other devices only proposed if they are needed.

Something tangible, like actual straw for the crib, little counters of different colours for the good acts (no counting of bad ones) is a help.

Hang a big card quite low in the class-room, with a suitable picture, and print in colours below :

THE GREAT DAY IS COMING

XV. SOME THOUGHTS WHICH MAY BE SUGGESTED

If we had been at Bethlehem on the first Christmas night, Our Lady might perhaps have let us hold the Infant Jesus in our arms for a moment. In Holy Communion we do more : we receive Him into our very hearts, and we can fancy Our Lady saying to us— " Take great care of my little Baby Jesus, and say something very loving to Him."

Our Guardian Angel follows us to the Communion rails. When we receive Holy Communion, he bows very low, and adores Our Blessed Lord, because He knows that He is truly God, but our Angel might well envy us, for we not only adore Him, but receive Him into our hearts.

We must ask Our Lady and our good Angel to teach us how to receive Him well.

Your soul is like a young plant—The plant needs the sun, so does your soul need Our Lord in Holy Communion.

As the plant gets life, strength, growth and food from the sun, so your soul . . .

Tell the story of the Manna, applying it to Holy Communion.*

Some Gospel Words which the children might think over and talk over in connection with Holy Communion.

Whenever helpful give the context shortly.

" Lovest thou Me?" (St. John, xxi, 15-18).

" Whom do you say that I am?" (St. Matt., xvi, 13).

" There was no room for them in the inn." (St. Luke, xi, 7).

" I will come and heal him." (St. Matt., viii, 7).

" I am not worthy." (St. Luke, vii, 7).

"A little while and you shall see Me." St. John, xvi, 16).

" Learn of Me." (St. Matt., xi, 29).

" I am the Good Shepherd." (St. John, x, 11).

* Exodus xvi., 1-36.

K

" I am the Life." (St. John, xi, 25).
and countless others.

XVI. HOW TO HEAR HOLY MASS

Guide the children to recognise the different sections of the Mass.

1. *The beginning.* The priest prays in preparation.

Suggest to the children some of the thoughts given in the " Children's Bread," Part I, or some of the " Child's Prayers to Jesus," by Father Roche. Or get them to choose one of their pictures to look at; or if they have a little Crucifix, they can look at that, and tell Jesus that they love Him.

2. Everybody stands up and they stand up too—like a regiment ready to fight for Our Lord—how are they going to fight?

3. They kneel down again. This is the time to *give.*

Our Lord is giving Himself for us, and to us.

What are we going to give Him? Get children's suggestions.

(Their love and some acts of self-conquest are indispensable).

Suggest that they can, if they like, say over

some of their poetry to Jesus, or tell Him some of the stories they like best. Our Lord will love to hear them.

(The essential point here is that they should " *be talking to Jesus.*" It does not, of course, matter if the poetry, etc., is pious or not. A mother loves to see her child doing anything it has been taught to do. Our Lord's love is better than that).

4. The bell rings, and all who are sitting kneel down.

The bell is to tell us that Our Lord will soon be here—we must get ready, and we must remember to pray for father and mother and all we love. This is the best time of all to pray for them—because the priest is praying for them, and Our Lord is doing so too.

5. The bell rings again; Our Lord is very near. We bow our head and say, "Jesus, I want You, come! come quickly!" (Get children's thoughts).

6. The bell rings three times. At the first time we look up : Jesus has come. The priest is holding Him in his hands—high up—for us to see, and we say lovingly : "My Lord and my God!" and bow our heads again.

Explain the second Elevation in a similar way.

7. Now Our Lord is on the altar, and we must not leave Him alone a minute. Talk to Him just as you like. You may talk to Him

about yourself, your home, your school, Himself, His goodness to us, all He has given us.

Talk over some of the things you know He did when on earth—Bethlehem or Egypt or Nazareth—or some of the wonderful things He did by the lake, or talk about the Cross, etc.

Pray for many things—for all you want, for all you love, for the dead that all their souls may go straight to Heaven.

Say one "Our Father" slowly.

8. *The bell rings again.* This is to tell us that Jesus is coming from the altar into our hearts. We try to be very quiet—inside as well as outside—and we repeat slowly and softly to ourselves, "Jesus is coming, Jesus is coming. Come, dear Jesus, come quickly into my poor little heart and make it your own home! You said when on earth: 'Let little children come to Me.' Lord, I, Your little child, come to You, I long for You. Come to me." The priest gives Our Lord to you and you hold Him tight. Keep very quiet, let Him talk to you first. If He is silent, it means He wants you to talk to Him.

9. *Thanksgiving after Communion.*

(Select from these points according to the children and circumstances.)

Give Our Lord a long, loving welcome, because you are so glad to see Him.

Ask Him to put His arms round you as He

used to put His arms round little children when on earth, and to love you as He did them.

Put both your hands into His and promise Him you will always love Him, and never do what He does not like.

Ask Him to put both His wounded hands on your head to bless and guide you.

Repeat several times : " Jesus, I love You," and tell Him why.

Tell Our Lord how many friends you have, but that He is your best friend, and then trust Him with all your secrets.

Ask Him for all you want. Tell Him you know He knows everything, that He can do everything, and that He loves you so that He will not refuse you anything. Pray for all you love.

Then thank Him over and over again,

    for coming down from Heaven to us,

    for loving us so much,

    for living on our altars,

    for coming to us in Holy Communion,

    for this visit He is now paying you,

    for all the care He takes of us,

    for giving us His Mother,

and for all the good things He is always giving us.

Before you leave the Church pay a little visit to Our Lady—tell Her about Our Lord's visit to you—ask Her to put Her arms round you too, and always to love you, as you promise always to love Her.

Teach carefully the Rule of Fasting before Holy Communion.

Also the fact that Our Lord wants us to receive Him every day if possible.

Explain the meaning of *Spiritual Communion.*

Advise the children to make one at every Mass when they cannot communicate sacramentally.

The best explanation is given by getting them to make one.

A helpful way is to ask them to shut their eyes, as they do for " Picture Composition " and then to make a picture of Our Lord and they themselves talking to Him.

(The pictures on p. 76 of the Children's Bread " are for this purpose, and are very suggestive).

XVII. WELCOME

The idea of " Welcome " is a very helpful
one for First Communicants.

Choose some examples from the Gospel
Story of the different welcomes Our Lord
received when on earth :

> The Welcome of Bethlehem.
> The Welcome of St. Mary Magdalene on
>   Easter Day.
> The Welcome of Zaccheus.
> The Welcome of Simon, the Pharisee.
> The Welcome of St. Martha.
> The Welcome of little children.

Get the children to choose what they will
do and say to welcome Our Lord when He
comes.

THE FAITH FOR CHILDREN

THE
Faith for Children

(FROM SEVEN TO FOURTEEN)

By
MARY EATON

RELIGIOUS OF THE SACRED HEART
Author of " The Little Ones "

ST. AUGUSTINE ACADEMY PRESS
HOMER GLEN, ILLINOIS

Nil Obstat

PATRITIUS CAN. McGETTIGAN
Censor Deputatus

Imprimatur

✠ HENRICUS
Epus. Tipasae

Edimburgi
die 25 Junii, 1925

CONTENTS

The Faith for Children

SECTION I.

THE ARTICLES OF THE CREED

THE FIRST ARTICLE.—God, The Creation, The Blessed Trinity.

Read Genesis Chap. I., 1-27.

Matter for Conversation.

1 We cannot think of a life without *things*, but if it were not for God, we should have no *things*.

2 Ten years ago I was nowhere; how is it I am here now?

3 Who is the only One, to Whom we can say: "You made me?"

4 Did anyone else ever do half as much for me?

5 The things we make, we have a right over; we can do what we like with them; but God made me: what then?

6 We love what we have made, especially if we have made it very beautifully; God made me, very beautifully: What then?

7 God did not make me so beautifully, for nothing. He has some work ready for me to do. I am bound to do it. Why?

A

8 A great King has many servants—only a few of them wait on the King himself; God is the King and I am one of the servants.

9 What is my work?

    (a) To learn about Him and so get to know Him.

    (b) To love Him (this is my chief work), and therefore talk to Him in prayer.

    (c) To do what He tells me, and when He forbids me to do anything, to obey.

10 Servants work for wages—so do God's servants. What wages? Heaven. That is the place God made me for.

The Blessed Trinity:

1 Our Lord's Baptism.

    A ceremony meaning Penance and sorrow for sin; of being an occasion of grace to persons receiving it; they were sorry and wanted to do better.

    Our Lord, of course, had no sin, but He bore ours for love of us, and He wanted to set an example.

2 Description of the Scene—(Matt. iii., 10-17; Mark i., 9; Luke iii., 21, 22).

    The Voice, was the Voice of God the Father.

    God the Son, made Man, was receiving the Baptism of St. John the Baptist.

St. John calls Our Lord : " The Lamb
of God, Who takes away the sins of
the World."

God the Holy Ghost was there in the
form of a Dove, hovering over the
Head of Our Lord.

Three Persons in one God.

3 The last verse of the " Tantum Ergo " in
English, and the liturgical ending :
" Through Our Lord Jesus Christ Thy
Son, Who livest and reignest, in the
unity of the Holy Ghost; One God
World without end," might also be used
to explain the doctrine.

THE SECOND ARTICLE OF THE CREED : THE
INCARNATION.

Catechism 28.

The Incarnation is a mystery ; a mystery of
Religion is something which we cannot understand, but which God says is true.

Q. 41.—" There are two Natures in Jesus
Christ."

" Nature " is not an easy word to understand. Look at this flower—you do not
expect it to walk—it is not its *nature* to ; this
dog—he cannot speak—it is not his *nature*.
But the flower smells sweet, because it is
its nature to—etc. Our nature makes us able
to do things—for instance, we cannot fly, for

that is not our nature, it is the nature of birds
—but we can—with our body, walk, eat, talk,
etc., and with our soul we can think, choose,
want, picture things that are not there, etc.
Now Our Lord, Who is God, wanted to be
just like us—He wanted to have the same
Nature. He wanted to *see*, just as we see,
with eyes. He wanted to hear the sound of
voices, of laughter, etc., to talk to children
and to others, just as we talk; and to will
and to choose and to long for things, just as
we do. And He could not do this, unless *He
took our nature*, that means became like us—
with a body and soul like ours—doing just
what ours does.

e.g.—Our Lord talking to His Mother at
Nazareth, working with St. Joseph, etc.

Our Lord hungry in the desert—(Matt.
iv., 2).

Our Lord tired—(John iv., 6), etc., etc.

Q. 40.—This wonderful thing—God taking
a Body and Soul like ours—has been given a
long name—it is called the INCARNATION—
which means God taking our Flesh and be-
coming a Man, having a Mother, like us. So
that God has not always been Man. Nearly
2000 years ago, He sent the Angel Gabriel to
Nazareth, to find out if Our Lady would be
His Mother, and you remember that She
said : " Yes."

Q. 42.—There is only One Person in Jesus Christ.

We say sometimes pointing to a stranger :
" Who is that person ?" When Our Lord was
on earth, anyone who did not know Who He
was might have pointed to Him and said :
" Who is that Person ?" The true answer
would have been, one little word : " GOD."
" God, the Second Person of the Blessed
Trinity." It was *God* Who was walking by
the lake ; God Who was born in Bethlehem ;
God, Who died on the Cross, etc. The God-
made-Man. No other Person—only God—
Who took our nature (we saw what that
meant) to be able to do what we did, and to
show us how much He loved us.   .

Q. 41.—So God Our Lord, the Second
Person of the Blessed Trinity, had two
Natures—the Nature of God—because He
was God and always had been God and
always would be God, and the Nature of Man,
which He took up, when He became Man,
nearly 2000 years ago.

On B.B.—ONE PERSON : THE SECOND
PERSON OF THE BLESSED TRINITY.

TWO NATURES : NATURE OF GOD (He
was God).

NATURE OF MAN (Body and Soul like
ours).

INCARNATION; God taking a Body and
  Soul like ours.

Whatever God the Father could do, God
the Son could do, because They are one and
the same God.

Example: The stilling of the Tempest
(Matt. viii., 18-28; Mark iv., 35-40; Luke viii.,
22-26).

Note especially :—

He slept because He was Man; He woke,
  when called, as Man.

He commanded the winds and waves as
  God; they obeyed Him, because He
  was God.

" What manner of Man is this?"
    Answer : The God-Man.

Q. 43.—Why God became Man. To redeem
    us from sin and hell.

Redeem means to buy back, *e.g.*, St.
Gregory wanted to buy back the Anglo-Saxon
slaves in the market-place in Rome.   He
made up his mind to redeem them from
slavery.

The 3rd, 4th, 5th, 6th, and 7th Articles of
the Creed require very little, if any, doctrinal
explanation.

The Gospel story should be told vividly and
made interesting by details, perhaps not yet
given.

Some are given below for reference.

Children of this age (probably seven or eight years old) are too young for any deeper teaching on the Holy Ghost (the Eighth Article), than what can be given by a vivid description of His Descent, on Whit Sunday. (And see " Little Ones," p. 55). All explanation of the Ninth Article should be deferred till later. (See Chap. III. and Chap. VI.).

SOME DETAILS ON THE SACRED PASSION.*

In all probability, Our Lord spent the Wednesday, before He suffered, in Bethany or on the Mount of Olives; He did not go to Jerusalem.

Some commentators say that He spent the night on the mountain-side, others, that He slept at Bethany, and probably Our Lady was there.

HOLY THURSDAY.—Early in the morning, the sentence of the "Greater Excommunication" was solemnly, and with sound of trumpet, pronounced by one of the Priests, against Jesus of Nazareth; this was to pave the way, as it were, for what was to follow.

St. Peter and St. John were sent by Our Lord to prepare the Pasch. He probably told

* See " Watches of the Passion." Fr. P. Gallwey, S. J. Manresa Press.

them to enter the City by the Southern Gate; that is where the water-carrier was.

A large Upper Room is still visited in Jerusalem, and called the "Coenaculum."

Tradition points to its being on the right spot; it is 40 feet long, and is rather like a little Church: an aisle and nave, with a row of pillars between the two.

When Our Lord reached the Garden of Olives, He pointed to a bed of hard, smooth rock, about two feet above the level of the ground, and told the eight Apostles to remain there, whilst He took Peter, James, and John with Him.

To reach the Grotto where He prayed, He had to descend some 27 steps, but it is but a "stone's cast" from the place where He left the three chosen ones.

The Grotto itself measures 40 feet by 30 feet, and is about 12 feet high.

Mass is said here constantly.

The Olive Gardens were irrigated by artificial means; most of the olives have disappeared.

Eight ancient olive trees, supported by masonry, and with a wall round them, still remain, and an uninterrupted tradition, traceable up to the third century, points them out as having been there the night Our Lord prayed.

At the Betrayal, the crowd of servants have clubs and lanterns or torches; the Roman soldiers wear swords.

It is thought that, when the Apostles fled, they chose the road on the left hand to the South; the caves in which they hid are still shewn.

The road along which Our Lord was dragged on His way to Annas is now called the Road of the Captivity; it is about a mile long.

THE NIGHT BETWEEN HOLY THURSDAY AND GOOD FRIDAY.

There was probably one gateway and one courtyard, common to the houses of Annas and Caiphas. Annas's house was to the left; Caiphas's was to the right, and the courtyard was between the two; there would be, of course, an entrance from each house, leading into it.

1 Coming from Gethsamene, they arrive first at the gateway, where the portress was.

2 They enter into a covered hall—the outer hall or vestibule in which is the porter's lodge : " before the Court."—(Mark xiv).

3 Passing on from the covered hall, they find themselves in the open courtyard, which was surrounded by a covered colonnade.

4 From this court a flight of steps led to the

Judgment Hall of the High Priest, and
Our Lord was led up these.

5 A fire was burning in the centre of the
courtyard, occasionally St. Peter found
a seat near it; at other times he had to
stand.

6 *Hours of St. Peter's Denial.* The first was
shortly after 1 a.m., the cocks having
been awakened by the noisy entrance of
the Cohort; the second about 1.45; the
third, with the second crowing at about
3 a.m.

7 The prison where Our Lord was kept during
the night was an underground dungeon;
in the middle of the rocky floor stood a
pillar 2 feet high; an iron ring was
attached to it, to which His wrists were
tightly tied. The door was locked and
barred, and Our Lord remained alone.

GOOD FRIDAY : "As soon as it was day."

1 The Meeting of the Sanhedrin was in the
Judgment Hall of Annas and Caiphas,
and was held about 6 a.m.

2 They then set out on their march from
Caiphas to Pilate's Palace. The Prætorium to which Our Lord was led was
not *within* the Palace, but in a separate
building at a much lower level.

On the northern side of the Prætorium there

was a large courtyard, paved with reddish stones, called the Lithostratos, " but
in Hebrew Gabbatha," where there was
a raised tribunal.

A balcony of the Palace overlooked the
Lithostrotos, to which it was connected
by a flight of marble steps, which are now
venerated in Rome as the Scala Sancta.

Pontius Pilate had then been about nine
years in office; he was the first Roman
General to quarter the Roman Cohorts
in the City and to order the Roman
Eagle to be displayed there. He had
taken money out of the Temple Treasury
for public works, and was therefore very
unpopular with the Jews.

3 When Our Lord reached Pilate's Judgment
Hall (the Prætorium) it must have been
about 7 a.m. After this first examination, Pilate, as we know, sent Our Lord
to Herod.

Herod's Palace was about ten minutes'
walk to the north of the Prætorium, in a
new part of the City; some of the road
must have been uphill.

4 When on Our Lord's return, Pilate could
" find no cause " in Our Lord, he said :
" I will chastise Him *therefore*."

THE SCOURGING.—By the law of Moses, 39
stripes was the limit; 13 on each shoulder,

and 13 on the chest. The Romans were not limited to any particular number. Two kinds of cords were used :—the Flagellum, made of several thin cords ; the Flagrum, made of one heavy lash.

The low pillar, to which Our Lord was tied for the Scourging, stood at the north side of the Lithostrotos, the side furthest removed from the Governor's House.

The Scourging, it is thought, lasted an hour.

Our Lord is said to have revealed to St. Bridget that the number of stripes was 5000.

The Crowning with Thorns.

A barrack yard was attached to the Lithostrotos, and according to tradition it was here that the soldiers led Our Lord, after the Scourging, to crown Him with thorns.

St. John and St. Mark say the mantle was purple ; St. Matthew says it was scarlet. The Greek word used means a red colour.

Some say the Crown was a kind of cap, which covered the whole Head ; others say a wreath.

After the Crowning, Pilate gave orders that the Prisoner should be brought to him.

The "Ecce Homo."

Pilate did not descend the Scala Sancta, but walked along a terrace to the balcony. He was attended by his own bodyguard, and a very large and angry crowd were gathered below. It is now about half-past ten a.m.

Our Lord is brought on to the balcony, and Pilate points to Him, as he says : "Behold the Man."

The great surging crowd, egged on by the priests, shout back: "Away with Him: Crucify Him !"

Pilate imposes silence and asks with a sneer : " Shall I crucify your King?" and the people, renouncing their nationality as well as their God, reply : " We have no King but Cæsar."

" Then Pilate delivered Him to be crucified."

A Pillar is pointed out in Jerusalem, in the " Via Crucis," called the " Pillar of the Sentence." It is thought that Pilate wrote his sentence, and that it was fastened to this stone.

The Via Crucis.

Jerusalem is cut as it were in two, from south to north, by a very narrow valley or gorge; no carriage road is therefore possible from east to west.

The Way of the Cross, about three quarters of a mile in length, starts from the Prætorium westward, down the incline into the gorge, and up a longer and steeper ascent to Calvary.

The streets leading from the bottom of the gorge to Calvary are *now* like a flight of broad steps or small terraces; horses, donkeys, and camels can go by them, but no carriages.

There are 130 steps from the bottom of the gorge to Calvary.

Tradition tells that St. Simon of Cyrene and his two sons were all three afterwards Bishops in Spain under St. James.

Three folds of St. Veronica's handkerchief are preserved; one in Rome, one in Jerusalem, and one in Spain. Her original name was Berenice, and she was a dear friend of Our Lady.

Our Lord met the Holy Women of Jerusalem at the junction of the two roads, the one leading N.-W. towards Gabaon, the other direct to Calvary.

CALVARY.

It can scarcely be called a hill; it is part of one of the five hills on which Jerusalem stands, called Gareb, and "the place of Calvary" stands on its very gentle slope. It is really a small plateau, raised about 20 feet above the ground around it. The whole hill is 50 or 60 feet at most.

On the east side of Calvary there is a deep precipice, part of the gorge, and it was here that St. Helen found the three crosses.

On the western side the descent is less steep, and about 90 feet from the Cross was St. Joseph of Arimathea's garden, with its sepulchre hewn out of the rock.

There is a tradition that Adam's skull was buried here, and that it was here that Abraham offered Isaac in sacrifice.

Four soldiers were told off for each of the Condemned. The tradition is that Our Lord was confined in a little cave on the left hand, below the level of Calvary, till all was ready. On its site now stands the chapel called: "The Prison of the Lord."

In the Church of the Holy Sepulchre, an altar is erected where Our Lord lay down on His Cross for Crucifixion, and another where the Cross was raised and planted in the rock. The Cross was probably 15 feet in length; certain early writers state that it was made of palm, olive, cedar and cypress wood.

Roman Law required that the crime of the crucified—" his cause "—should appear over his head. The Title was written in red characters on a board whitened with lime. It was probably fastened to the Cross *after* Our Lord had been crucified. A portion of this board, with the characters upon it, is still shown in the Church of the Holy Cross of Jerusalem in Rome.

The eclipse was really general; St. Denis the Areopagite says that he saw it at Heliopolis; the Fathers say that the earthquake was also felt throughout the world. A fissure in the rock on Calvary is still pointed out; tradition says it opened between the Cross of Christ and that of the impenitent Thief.

THE BURIAL.

The Jews carried lighted torches, when they accompanied the dead body to the grave.

The Tomb of Our Lord was hewn out of the rock, with an upright doorway between 3 and 4 feet high.

At the time of the Burial there was an ante-chamber about a yard in depth, and then an inner chamber, entered by this low door. The inner chamber or Tomb, where Our Lord was laid, is about 9 feet in depth and 7 feet in length; the height is about 9 feet.

The stone bed on which Our Lord's Body was laid is on the right hand of the entrance door, along the wall of the chamber as you enter.

One of the Fathers tells us : " He had not been dead more than seven minutes before they pierced His side and Dismas died."

Joseph and Nicodemus arrived about 3.30 p.m.

At 5 p.m. they laid Him in the Tomb.

At 5.30 p.m. they rolled the stone to the door of the Sepulchre.

At 7.30 p.m. Our Lady and St. John reached the Coenaculum.

> For further details, see "The Watches of the Passion" (Vol. II.—Father Gallwey), from which much of the above is taken.

TENTH ARTICLE OF THE CREED : THE FORGIVENESS OF SIN.

Teach Actual Sin before Original Sin.

Q. 114.—Tell the story of the Paralytic.—Matt. xi., 1, 2, 6 to 12; verses 3, 4, and 5 better omitted at this stage.

Apply to the Sacrament of Penance.

Q. 111.—Christ has left to His Church the power of forgiving sin.

To have *Power* means "to be able to do" (cf., a powerful machine, man, etc.). Our Lord wanted the people to be quite sure that He had the power to forgive sins, and so He worked a great miracle that they could all see, to prove it.

"The Son of Man (one of Our Lord's favourite names for Himself) has power on earth to forgive sins."

B

Christ has left this power to His Church.
Supposing you had been very naughty and
your father had punished you by locking you
into a room; later, he might go himself and
unlock the door and let you out—(Our Lord
Himself forgave the paralytic); or he might
give the key to your eldest brother and say:
"Go and let him out; tell him I have forgiven him." (Apply this to the Pastors of
Christ's Church).

Q. 119.—Sin—is an Offence against God.

Sin is doing what we know God does not
want us to do = DEED.

Sin is saying what we know God does not
like = WORD.

Sin is thinking what we know God tells us
not to think = THOUGHT.

Sin is saying: "Yes, I know God wants me
to do this, but I am not going to do it"
(OMISSION). We *omit* it; leave it undone.

These are Actual Sins; things we actually
do—actions of our own. When we *choose* to
be disobedient to God, we sin. God wants us
to speak the truth and we choose to tell a lie.
God wants us to be patient and kind, and we
are angry and unkind, and we *mean it;* then
we sin—we offend God; we wound Our
Lord's Sacred Heart; we hurt ourselves too,
the best part of ourselves—our souls.

Qs. 120 and 121.—Mortal Sin. There are big sins and smaller sins.

Story of Cain and Abel: a big sin.— (Genesis iv., 1-16).

1 Cain at work in the fields; Abel taking care of the sheep. (Show Picture).

2 The Sacrifice. The smoke of Abel's sacrifice ascends; that of Cain is driven back. (Compare with smoke of incense at Benediction).

Describe the two brothers as they turn away from the sacrifice. Abel looked as people do coming back from Holy Communion; Cain angry, with black looks, and no prayer on his lips, muttering to himself.

God speaks to Cain's heart; tells him he has sinned by hating Abel, and that is why the smoke will not go up straight to heaven: tells him too that if he will give up sinning and do good, it *will* be accepted—but Cain will not listen.

Cain makes up his mind to murder his brother. He *chooses* the evil thing.

He asks Abel to come out for a walk in the fields, and when they are there, he suddenly turns upon him, throws him down—he is the stronger of the two—and kills him. When he has done the deed, he gives one glance at the dead face of his brother, and with a cry of horror, flees away.

5 Eve misses both her sons. She goes out to
    seek them and finds the dead body of
    Abel lying on the ground. Adam, too,
    draws near, and looks at his son, slain by
    Cain, his eldest born.

These big sins are called *mortal*. We talk
of mortal illness—mortal wound—meaning
one that kills—takes away life.

Qs. 122 and 123.—What does mortal sin
kill? It kills the beautiful life we are now
leading with God. It kills our chances of
Heaven. It takes away all the beauty of our
souls, just as some very bad illnesses take
away all the beauty of our body.

If a man ran a knife through anyone's
heart, he would kill the life of his body, so
those who commit a big sin, such as Cain's,
run, as it were, a knife through their soul and
kill it. Mortal sin makes God turn away:
the grace has gone and life has gone too.

**Qs. 124 and 125.—Where will they go who
die in Mortal Sin?**

If we committed a big sin like that, God
would be so displeased with us, that if we
died with it on our souls, He would shut the
gates of Heaven and not let us in. We should
be like Cain, cast away from God. We should
have no home to go to and we should be
punished in a place called Hell, for ever and
ever.

Our Lord, when He was on earth, often spoke to the people about Hell. He said it had been got ready for the devils—not for us (Matt. v., 29), but that those who on earth did not love Him would go there too; that there was there a terrible fire, always burning; that it was quite dark, and that everyone wept there (Matt. viii., 12), and that all this came of *doing what they chose,* instead of what He told them.

He warned the people too that Hell was the only thing they need fear—it did not really matter (Our Lord said) if we were blind in this life, if only we saw Him in Heaven, or if we had only one hand on earth, if only we got safe to Heaven (Matt. xviii., 8, 9, and Chap. v., 29); that it was better not to have too much of the good things in this world and to get all good things in the next. And when He had taught all this, He asked them: "Have you understood all these things?" because it was so important that we should understand, and because Our Lord was so anxious to keep us from Hell.

It is unwise to play on the children's imagination about Hell, and there is no need, for the facts are enough, and our Lord has told us all we need to know.

Impress:

1 Those who on earth do not love Our Lord

go to Hell, like the devils for whom it
was prepared.

2 A terrible fire is always burning there and
will never be put out.

3 It is always dark, and everyone weeps
there.—(St. Matt. xxii., 13, and xxv.,
30).

Q. 123.—" Sanctifying Grace is the super=
natural life of the soul."

Sanctifying Grace is the name of one of
God's most beautiful gifts to us. He gave it
us at Baptism. It shines in our souls, making
them all golden and filling them with life. As
long as this golden light shines in our souls
God loves to look on them; mortal sin puts
the light out and God turns away.

Examples of evil:—Home burnt down; loss
of those we love best; if we could never walk
about or were blind or deaf, etc. But sin,
i.e., choosing what God has forbidden, is a
far greater evil than those.

Supposing that after our house had been
burnt down, a very kind, rich friend said:
" Never mind, I will build it up again for
you, and make it far more beautiful than
before, and I will put into this new home
everything you ask me for, and he did it;
and then we went to live in this beautiful
home, how much we should love him and how
grateful we should be !

But suppose when we arrived at our new home, we found the door locked and we could not get in, and our kind friend was very angry with us, and he turned us away, and we never had a home again, that would be a great evil surely, far greater than the first.

LAZARUS AND DIVES.—(Luke xvi., 1-23).
(Not the remaining verses).

Our Lord told the people too of a rich man He had known called Dives. This man was always beautifully dressed; every meal he had was a feast, and he had more money than he knew what to do with. He lived in a beautiful palace; a long flight of white marble steps lead up to the big entrance, and on these cold steps lay a poor beggar called Lazarus, who was very ill. He was covered with terrible sores and he was starving.

He asked the rich man as he passed out of his beautiful palace on his way to the city, to let him have some of the crumbs that fell from his table, but Dives drew his grand clothes round him lest they should touch the poor beggar; he shuddered at the sight of his sores and passed on quickly without giving him anything. This was very wicked, and God was very much displeased. Dives went on from bad to worse, forgetting God, and doing many wrong things. Then he died, and

Our Lord Who knew all things, and Who was his Judge, told the people that he went to Hell. And poor Lazarus who had all the bad things of this world, and who had loved God all the time, and been patient and good, one day saw a troop of Angels coming to fetch him to Heaven. One of them stooped over him so gently and lovingly, and raised him in his arms, and all the pain ceased and all the sores were healed, and Our Lord told the people that the Angels carried him to Heaven.

Do you remember Our Lord said that it was better for us to be lame and blind in this world than to have good things?

Q. 126.—Venial Sin.—The *habit* of venial sin which may lead to mortal sin should be dwelt on—*e.g.*, Judas—he began by small thefts, etc.

Venial means " pardonable." The Roman Pardon was called a Venia—hence the word.

Qs. 114, 115 and 116.—Original Sin.— A certain rich man had a large family, many sons and daughters. He was the servant of a great King, who had given him a beautiful home to live in, and many precious things besides. One evil day this servant was tempted to betray his King and turn traitor, so as to get all the Kingdom for himself. The King was very angry, and ordered the wicked servant and his wife and sons and daughters to be put to death. But the servant was now very sorry for what he had done, and his wife, who had urged her husband to betray the King, now wept bitterly. So the King ordered that, instead of being put to death, they should all be banished from their beautiful home and never enter it again.

The sons and daughters had *not* betrayed their King, but because their father and mother had committed this great crime, the whole family was exiled and disgraced; the sons and daughters were banished too, and no one who bore their name was ever again to enter the beautiful palace which had once been theirs.

The children can be led to see that the servant is Adam, his wife Eve—*We* (this is the point) are their children, and we were disgraced and exiled through the sin of Adam and Eve, until Our Blessed Lord, the King's only Son, took away our disgrace and sentence of exile, by *redeeming us*, paying the price for us to our Heavenly Father, when He died on the Cross.

Make it clear that "the guilt and stain of Original Sin" is very different from "the guilt and stain of Actual Sin." The former is our misfortune—just as we might contract a disease from someone. The latter is our

fault. Through the former we *lost* something
very precious—just as if our father was out of
work or lost some money, we should become
poor too.   For the latter *we are punished*,
because we alone are to blame.

Qs. 117 and 118.—Immaculate Conception.
—Our Lord redeemeth us all, but He redeemed Our Lady more perfectly than anyone else, because She was His Mother. If two
children are in danger of falling, the mother
catches one in her arms and prevents its falling—the other falls and hurts itself; the
mother then cures the hurt. God caught Our
Lady in His Arms, as it were, *before* She
could fall; Our Lord saved us *after*.

N.B.—The name " Immaculate Conception " should be taught *as a name*.

The Sacrament of Penance
Necessity of Confession

1 Teach the obligation clearly and distinctly.

i. We are bound to confess once a year.

ii. If we had the terrible misfortune to
do anything very wrong, we are
bound to confess it, and it is well to
do so as soon as we can, because we
want God's friendship, and whilst we
are in mortal sin we are in terrible
danger of Hell.

iii. People who are dying must go to Confession if they are able.

iv. Our Lord wants us, if possible, to receive Him in Holy Communion every day. Our hearts must be kept pure for Him, so it is well to go to Confession once a fortnight.

Do not let the children think that Confession is a necessary preparation for Holy Communion. This is quite contrary to the mind of the Church (except, of course, for those who have had the misfortune to fall into mortal sin).

A child goes to Confession; he has God's grace in his soul, but he has done several things that are wrong (venial sins). He is sorry and he tells the priest all about it. The priest says : "I absolve thee from thy sins." At that moment those sins disappear, the Precious Blood is poured on him, and he comes away with his soul far more beautiful than it was before. He has got more grace, and therefore more love of God, and God loves him more. Therefore, we should go to Confession regularly once a fortnight.

Contrition—another name for sorrow; it means a rending or tearing, and sorrow, as it were, does this to our hearts.

We may have many reasons for being sorry. A man may have stolen some money; he is caught, and put in prison and kept there—he has time to think.

1 He is sorry because he hates being in prison —he hates the punishment he has got.

2 He is sorry because he has brought disgrace on himself; it is a shameful thing to be a thief.

3 He is sorry because his wife and children are very unhappy at home, and all because of him. And then he turns to God and prays; and

4 He is sorry because he knows God is displeased with him, and that if he dies as he is now he will lose his soul.

5 He thinks of Our Lord dying on the Cross for him, and he is more sorry still.

6 He thinks of all God has done for him, and of how good and beautiful God is, and of how God hates sin, and this makes him most sorry of all.

Show how motives 1, 2 and 3 are not contrition, because they have nothing to do with God; 5 and 6 are more unselfish than 4, and so illustrate the difference between perfect and imperfect contrition. Impress on children the importance of making daily acts of contrition, so that they may always have sorrow for sin in their hearts. Even if this contrition is imperfect, it is sufficient with the

priest's absolution, to wipe away all sin, and
thus secure Heaven to a poor sinner, who
through accident, or through a stroke, etc.,
becomes unconscious before the priest arrives.
Habitual sorrow for sin in a beautiful grace,
which we can obtain by frequent acts of contrition.

CONDITIONS OF FORGIVENESS.

1 God says He will not forgive unless the person who did the wrong is sorry.
2 He says too, that if we have done something very wrong we must confess it.
God will forgive us as soon as we are
sorry, but He insists on our going to Confession and owning what we have done,
if it is something very wrong.
3 God says He will not forgive us unless we
make up our minds never to do this
wrong thing again. If we do not promise
to try never to do it again, we are not
really sorry.

It is very easy to get God's forgiveness.
He is always anxious to forgive, and He never
keeps us waiting. As soon as we say we are
sorry and promise never to do it again, God
makes it all right, just as it was before we
have done it, only we have one more reason
for loving Him dearly.

Tell the story of St. Mary Magdalen.—
(Luke vii., 37-50).

PREPARATION FOR CONFESSION

(For a very simple preparation and Thanksgiving for Confession see " The Little Ones,"
p. 108).

1 " Lord that I may see."—(Luke xviii., 41).
  What?
    How bad sin is.
    How good You are.

2 What have I done that You, my God, do
  not like ?
    In the morning ?   Afternoon ?   Even-
      ing ?
    On Sundays ?   On week-days ?
    At home ?   At school ?
    What have I done that my parents do
      not like ?
    What have I done that my companions
      do not like ?
    Did You, Lord, dislike it too ?
    Did I listen to my Guardian Angel and
      do what he said ?

This is what the Catechism calls " Examination of Conscience "—turning over in our
mind what we have done, to see if it is all
right.

3 Jesus, my God, I love You, because You
    are so good.   I am very sorry that I have
    done this——and this——and this, which
    You dislike, and I will not do it any
    more.   Shut your eyes and picture Our

Lord hanging on the Cross, and you yourself kneeling at its foot. This will help
you to be sorry.

4 *Think:* Why did I do it? This may help
you to avoid it next time.

Ask Our Lady to help you to tell the priest
exactly and shortly what you have done,
and to make you more sorry than you
are.

Your Angel Guardian goes with you to the
Confessional, and he will help you too.

FORMULA FOR CONFESSION.

Little children will of course make very
informal Confessions, and this is well, but
later on, the proper simple framework should
be used, and a certain amount of " drilling "
is required to teach it.

" Pray, Father, give me your blessing,
for I have sinned."

" My last Confession was a fortnight ago.
Since then———

" For these and all other sins that I cannot now remember, I am heartily
sorry, purpose amendment, and beg
penance and Absolution of you,
Father."

HOLY COMMUNION.

For preparation for First Communion, see
" The Little Ones," pp. 121-137.

Q. 129.—The Resurrection of the Body.

1 Tell the story of Our Lord's Apparition on what we now call "Low Sunday," to the Apostles, including St. Thomas.—(John xx., 24-29).

Bring out that:

    i. Our Lord's Body had been taken down from the Cross on Good Friday, and His Soul had gone to Limbo. Death is the separation of body and soul. A dead body cannot move, because it has no life.

    ii. On Easter Sunday He joined His Body to His Soul again.

Get from the children, by reference to the Apparition, some of the results of this: the passing through the closed doors, etc. Dwell on the fact that it was evidently the same Body: the marks of the Wounds in His Hands, Feet and Side, *prove* this beyond a doubt.

What Our Lord did for Himself on Easter Day, He will do for each of us, *some* day.

We call that day the Day of Judgment, because Our Lord has promised—and He always keeps His promise—to come back again to this, our earth, to judge the good and the wicked. And He said that "all that are in the grave (that is you and I, and everyone that has died) shall hear the voice of the Son of God. And they that have done good things shall come forth unto the resurrection of life."—(John v., 28, 29).

Our Lord meant that our bodies shall rise when He calls them, just as the body of Lazarus rose, when He said : " Come forth." But there is a great difference, for Lazarus's body remained mortal, and he had to die again. Our bodies, when Our Lord calls us, will be immortal, beautiful, glorious.

Revise the Seventh Article of the Creed.

Give a graphic rendering of St. Matthew, chap. xxv., verses 31-46.

Qs. 131 and 134.—Where shall we go when we die?

We have seen that there is one place that we must never go *near*—Hell; that there is only one thing that can take us there—a big sin, and we must pray every day to God to keep us from sin, and to stop us when we want to sin. It all depends on what we choose. No one can make us sin, no one can stop us from sinning, unless we *choose*.

We must never forget that sin is the road to Hell.

Jesus keep me from sin—keep me from all that offends You.

So, when we die, we are going to Heaven. We have quite made up our minds about that.

c

But this might happen. You know every sin, even a small one is punished, and it may be that when we die we shall have some small sins on our soul, or God might see that we had not done penance for all our past sins.

Then we could not go *straight* to Heaven— we are not quite ready, for souls even with a little speck on them are not quite ready for Heaven.

If we had got our clothes torn and dirty, we should have to wait till they were clean and mended, before we went to see the King and Queen.

Fortunately there is a place where we can get little sins removed, and where we can do all the penance we ought to have done on earth. Purgatory means a cleansing place. If we go there we shall have great pain, but it will not last for ever, and we are sure of Heaven at the end.

It would be ever so much better to do our penance here, but what we have not done, *must* be done in Purgatory.

There are people in Purgatory now, at this very moment, and we can help them by asking God to lessen and shorten their pain. A tiny prayer, *e.g.*, " My Jesus Mercy !" will do this for the " Holy Souls," so called, because they are so near to God and quite sure of Heaven.

Qs. 132 and 133.—Heaven! That will come as soon as ever Purgatory is over. Our Lord has told us how He will receive us when we arrive. He will say that glad little word: "Come!" He will call us "Blessed," and He will tell us that because on earth we have done the few things He asked, He is now going to give us many things. We are to have the same joy as He has for ever and ever!— (Matt. xxv., 21, 23). He will give us each a place in Heaven (Matt. xxv., 34) which He Himself has prepared for us (John xiv., 2), and He will give us a Kingdom where we shall reign.

All that Our Lord possesses will be ours: Our Lord promised this.—(Matt. xxiv., 47; Ap. vii., 10). We shall never be hungry or thirsty in Heaven, but we can have beautiful banquets whenever we like (Luke xii., 37), and sit at Our Lord's own table.—(Luke xxii., 30).

We shall see Our Lord in His beauty and in our own true home, which seems now so far away.—(Isaias xxxiii., 17).

We shall never cry any more, because God Himself has promised to wipe away all our tears.—(Ap. xxi., 4).

We shall never be sad again.—(Isa. lx., 18).

The very moment we want a thing we shall have it.

When we find things here are hard, we must remember that we have " a better, a heavenly country " which is coming (Heb. xi., 16), and that Heaven is our true home.

" Eye hath not seen nor ear heard, neither hath it entered into the heart of man to conceive, what things God hath prepared for them that love Him."—(I. Cor., ii., 9).

The children may perhaps not understand, without help, what St. Paul means : " However beautiful, splendid, happy, delightful, we imagine Heaven to be, God says it is a thousand times more beautiful and splendid, a thousand times happier and more delightful than that. So that whatever we think of Heaven, we can always say : " Better still ! "

DEVOTION TO THE SACRED HEART

Set before the children a picture of Our Lord pointing to His Heart.

This is a picture of Our Lord and He is God. Why is He pointing to His Heart?

It is with our hearts that we love, so what does this remind us of?

What do the flames coming from His Heart recall to us?

" O Sacred Heart of Jesus, burning with love for me. Inflame my heart with love for Thee."

THE FAITH FOR CHILDREN 87

See—It is surmounted by a cross.

It is surrounded by thorns.

It is pierced through.

What does all this tell us?

When was Our Lord's Heart pierced?

Recall the words: " Greater love than this hath no man, that he lay down his life for his friend."

Our Lord is the only one who has given His life for me.

Why did He give His life?

What did He save me from?

1 Get the children to make as complete a list as they can of all that Our Lord has done for us; be sure they include—the Gift of the Blessed Sacrament, Holy Mass, the Faith given to them, good parents, etc.

2 Tell the story of the picture in which Our Lord holds His Heart in His left Hand, and stretches out the pierced right Hand, as if begging.

[The artist prayed long before the Blessed Sacrament, asking how he should paint Our Lord's picture. As he left the Church, a poor beggar, with one hand over his heart, and the other stretched out appealingly, begged for an alms—the painter took this as an answer to his prayer].

In the picture what is Our Lord asking for ?
What is He offering us ?

Note that He is offering His whole Heart.
What must we give Him ?

He wants us to return Him love for love,
and He has shewn us how we can do that.—
" If you love Me, keep My commandments."
(Develop this point).

3 Besides the Commandments of God and of
   the Church, Our Lord said :

> "A new Commandment I give unto
> you, that you love one another, as I
> have loved you ";

> " By this shall all men know that you
> are My disciples, if you have love one
> for another ";

And again :

> " Whatsoever you do to the least of
> these, you do it to Me ";

And again Our Lord said :

> " Learn of Me who am meek and
> humble of heart."

So He wants us to imitate Him in His
meekness, gentleness, patience. The children
should give examples shewing when Our Lord
practised these virtues, and how they could
practise them themselves.

We can also show Our Lord how much we
love Him by trusting Him with all our little
troubles and difficulties. He loves us to tell

Him all about them, and He will help us as He alone can. And lastly, we can show our love by trying to console Our Lord in all *His* troubles, which are caused by the sins of wicked people. This is called: "making reparation."

Here are some ways of making reparation, and you can think of others :—

    i. To offer the Holy Mass. Why is this the best of all ways?

    ii. To offer Him our Communions in reparation.

    iii. Visits to the Blessed Sacrament, when we can talk to Him of all the things which give Him pain.

    iv. Denying ourselves; doing hard things which cost, to make up to Our Blessed Lord, for all His pain.

    v. Making acts of reparation :—

        " Jesus, meek and humble of heart, etc.

        " O Sacred Heart of Jesus, may Thy kingdom come !"

        " Sacred Heart of Jesus, have mercy on all poor sinners."

        " Sacred Heart of Jesus, I put my trust in Thee."

This lesson might be supplemented by others :—

i. A very simple account of the apparitions of Our Lord to St. Margaret Mary.

ii. An explanation of the acts of reparation and of—

    (a) The institution of the Feast. (Make clear as to its position in the Liturgical Year).

    (b) Holy Hour : when and how made.

    (c) The devotion of the nine First Fridays and of the Badge.

iii. The Enthronement of the picture of the Sacred Heart in the home.

iv. The Promises made by the Sacred Heart to those who love Him.

SECTION II.

THE COMMANDMENTS

(This matter may be taught, before or after the Sacraments—see Section IV.—according to the Syllabus followed).

Q. 169, 170, 171—The Greatest Command= ment: Charity

Teach Matt. xvii., 35-39. Also Luke x., 30-37.

These two scenes, given as stories, will be sufficient to illustrate and explain what Charity is.

(a) Bring the children's thoughts back to the Last Supper. Note what Our Lord's love that night had made Him do. He expected the Apostles and us to love Him in return and He asked for *One* and only one proof of love. "If you love Me, do what I tell you to do."

(b) Make the children understand the big

principle, that we never obey anyone but
God—when we do what our Superiors tell
us, it is *only* because God is telling us
through them. This principle should
stand by them for life.

Catechism Answer **173** should be learnt
after the Commandments have been taught.

Q. 172—The Giving of the Commandments

The story of Moses, of the Deliverance of
the Hebrews, the giving of the Ten Commandments on Mount Sinai should be told as
graphically as possible and in their right
geographical setting; using the actual words
of Scripture whenever possible.

I.—Moses's Mission.

"Now Moses fed the sheep of Jethro, his
father-in-law, and he drove the flock to the
inner parts of the desert, and came to the
mountain of God, Horeb. And the Lord
appeared to him in a flame of fire out of the
midst of a bush, and he saw that the bush
was on fire and was not burnt. And Moses
said : "I will go and see this great sight, why
the bush is not burnt." And when the Lord
saw, that he went forward to see, He called
to him out of the midst of the bush, and said :
"Moses, Moses !"
And he answered : "Here I am."

And He said :

" Come not nigh hither, put off the shoes from thy feet : for the place whereon thou standest is holy ground. I am the God of thy fathers, the God of Abraham, the God of Isaac and the God of Jacob."

Moses hid his face, for he durst not look at God. And the Lord said to him :

" I have seen the affliction of My people in Egypt, and I have heard their cry because of the rigour of them that are over the works, and knowing their sorrow I am come down to deliver them out of the hands of the Egyptians and to bring them out of that land into a good and spacious land, into a land that floweth with milk and honey."

" But come, I will send thee to Pharoa, that thou mayst bring forth My people, the children of Israel out of Egypt."

And Moses said to God :

" Who am I that I should go to Pharoa, and should bring forth the children of Israel out of Egypt ?"

And He said to him :

" I will be with thee . . . I AM WHO AM. Thus shalt thou say to the children of Israel : ' HE WHO IS, hath sent me to you.'

" But I know that the King of Egypt will not let you go, but by a mighty hand. For I will stretch forth My Hand and will strike

Egypt with all My wonders, which I will do
in the midst of them : after these, he will let
you go." (Exodus iii., 1-8 ; 10-14 ; 19-21).

II.—AARON IS APPOINTED TO HELP HIM.

And the Lord said to Aaron :

" Go into the desert to meet Moses."

And he went forth to meet him in the
mountain of God and kissed him. And Moses
told Aaron all the words of the Lord by which
He had sent him and the signs He had commanded. And they came together and they
assembled all the Ancients of the children of
Israel. And Aaron spoke all the words which
the Lord had said to Moses, and he wrought
the signs before the people. And the people
believed, and they heard that the Lord had
visited the children of Israel and that He had
looked upon their affliction : and falling down
they adored. (Exodus iv., 27-31).

III.—PHAROA REFUSES TO LET THE PEOPLE GO.

After these things Moses and Aaron went
in and said to Pharoa :

" Thus saith the Lord God of Israel : ' Let
My people go that they may sacrifice to Me
in the desert.' "

But he answered :

" Who is the Lord that I should hear His
voice ? and let Israel go ? I know not the
Lord, neither will I let Israel go."

And they said :

" The God of the Hebrews hath called us, to go three days' journey into the wilderness and to sacrifice to the Lord our God, lest a pestilence or the sword fall upon us."

The King of Egypt said to them :

" Why do you, Moses and Aaron draw off the people from their works? Get you gone to your burdens."—(Exodus v., 1-4).

IV.—SIGNS AND WONDERS.

And the Lord said to Moses and Aaron :

" When Pharoa shall say to you. ' Shew signs '; thou shalt say to Aaron : ' Take thy rod and cast it down before Pharoa, and it shall be turned into a serpent.' "

So Moses and Aaron went in unto Pharoa and did as the Lord had commanded. And Aaron took the rod before Pharoa and his servants, and it was turned into a serpent. And Pharoa called the wise men and the magicians, and they also by Egyptian enchantments and certain secrets did in like manner. And they everyone cast down their rods, and they were turned into serpents; but Aaron's rod devoured their rods. And Pharoa's heart was hardened and he did not hearken to them.—(Exodus vii., 8-13).

Thus therefore said the Lord :

" In this thou shalt know that I am the

Lord; behold I will strike with the rod that is in my hand·the water of the river, and it shall be turned into blood; and the fishes that are in the river shall die, and the waters shall be corrupted, and the Egyptians shall be afflicted when they drink the water of the river."

And Moses and Aaron did as the Lord had commanded, and lifting up the rod he struck the water of the river before Pharoa and his servants, and it was turned into blood. And the fishes that were in the river died and the river corrupted, and the Egyptians could not drink the water of the river, and there was blood in all the land of Egypt.—(Exodus vii., 17-21).

And the Lord said to Moses :

"Go into Pharoa and thou shalt say to him : "Thus saith the Lord : Let my people go to sacrifice to Me. But if thou wilt not let them go, behold I will strike all thy coasts with frogs; and the river shall bring forth an abundance of frogs, which shall come up and enter into thy house and thy bed-chamber and upon thy bed . . . and into thy ovens and into the remains of thy meats."

And Aaron stretched forth his hand upon the waters of Egypt and the frogs came up and covered the land. But Pharoa called Moses and Aaron, and said to them :

" Pray ye to the Lord to take away the
frogs from me and from my people, and I will
let the people go to sacrifice to the Lord."

And Moses said : " I will do according to
thy word, that thou mayest know that there
is none like to the Lord our God." And the
Lord did according to the word of Moses, and
the frogs died out of the houses and out of
the villages and out of the fields. And they
gathered them together into immense heaps
and the land was corrupted.

And Pharoa seeing that rest was given
hardened his own heart, and did not hear
them, as the Lord had commanded.—(Exodus
viii., 1-8).

And God struck the Israelites with many
other plagues, and still Pharoa would not let
them go.

And the Lord said to Moses :

" Stretch out thy hand towards heaven,
and may there be darkness upon the land of
Egypt, so thick that it may be felt." And
Moses stretched forth his hand towards
heaven, and there came horrible darkness in
all the land of Egypt for three days. No
man saw his brother nor moved himself out
of the place where he was, but wheresoever
the children of Israel dwelt, there was light.
And Pharoa said to Moses :

" Get thee from me, and beware thou see

not my face any more; in what day soever
thou shalt come in my sight, thou shalt die."

And Moses answered :

" So shall it be as thou hast spoken. I will
not see thy face any more."

And it came to pass at midnight, the Lord
slew every first-born in the land of Egypt,
from the first-born of Pharoa who sat upon
his throne unto the first-born of the captive
woman that was in the prison, and all the
first-born of cattle. And Pharoa arose in the
night, and all his servants and all Egypt.
And there arose a great cry in Egypt, for
there was not a house wherein there lay not
one dead. And Pharoa calling Moses and
Aaron in the night, said :

"Arise and go forth from among my people,
you and the children of Israel; go, sacrifice
to the Lord as you say; your sheep and herds
take along with you as you demanded, and
departing, bless me."

And the Egyptians pressed the people to go
forth out of the land speedily, saying : " We
shall all die."

And when Pharoa had sent out the people,
the Lord led them about by the way of the
desert, which is by the Red Sea; and the Lord
went before them to shew the way, by day in
a pillar of a cloud, by night in a pillar of fire;
there never failed the pillar of the cloud by

day, nor the pillar of fire by night.—(Exodus
x., 21-24; xi., 29-33; xiii., 18, 21, 22).

And Pharoa and his servants said : "What
meant we to do that we let Israel go from
serving us ?"

So he made ready his chariot and took all
his people with him, all the chariots that were
in Egypt, and the captains of the whole army,
and he pursued the children of Israel, but
they were gone forth in a mighty hand. And
when the Egyptians followed they found them
encamped at the seaside. And when Pharoa
drew near, the children of Israel lifting up
their eyes saw the Egyptians behind them,
and they feared exceedingly, and cried to the
Lord. And Moses said to the people : "Fear
not. Stand and see the great wonders of the
Lord which He will do this day, for the
Egyptians whom you see now, you shall see
no more for ever."

And the Lord said to Moses :

" Lift thou up thy rod and stretch forth
thy hand over the sea and divide it, that the
children of Israel may go through the midst
of the sea on dry ground."

And when Moses had stretched forth his
hand over the sea the Lord took it away by
a strong and burning wind and turned it into
dry ground, and the water was divided. And
the children of Israel went in through the

D

midst of the sea dried up, for the water was as a wall on their right hand and on their left. And the Egyptians pursuing went in after them, and all Pharoa's chariots and horsemen, through the midst of the sea. And now the morning watch was come, and behold the Lord looking upon the Egyptian army through the pillar of fire and the pillar of cloud slew their host. And the Egyptians said: "Let us flee from Israel, for the Lord fighteth for them against us."

And the Lord said to Moses:

"Stretch forth thy hand over the sea that the waters may come again upon the Egyptians, upon their chariots and horsemen." And when Moses had stretched forth his hand towards the sea, it returned at the first break of day to the former place, and as the Egyptians were fleeing away the waters came upon them, and the Lord shut them up in the middle of the waves.—(Exodus xiv., 5-27).

After wandering in the desert for about three months, they came to Mount Sinai.

This desert, where the Israelites were for over a year, is really a continuation of the Sahara—a great desert belt, with a few valleys and old water-courses, called "wadis," date palms, acacia groves, and gum-trees scattered here and there. The whole mountainous mass of granite about

Sinai is called Horeb. Sinai is an individual peak (its name means the " Mountain of God "), with a fortress-like monastery of St. Catherine at its foot, a short distance above the Chapel of Elias, and on its summit, a little pilgrim Church—the whole stern and treeless in appearance.

Draw sketch of mountain and surrounding country on B.B.

"And Moses went up to God, and God called unto him from the mountain and said :

" You have seen what I have done to the Egyptians, how I have carried you upon the wings of eagles, and have taken you to Myself. If therefore you will hear My voice, you shall be my peculiar possession above all people."

And all the people answered together :

"All that the Lord hath spoken, we will do."

And the Lord said :

" Let them be ready against the third day ; for on the third day the Lord will come down in the sight of all the people upon Mount Sinai."

And now the third day was come, and the morning appeared, and behold thunders began to be heard, and lightning to flash, and a very thick cloud to cover the mountain, and the noise of the trumpet sounded exceedingly

loud; and the people that was in the camp
feared. And when Moses had brought them
forth to meet God from the place of the camp,
they stood at the bottom of the mount. And
all Mount Sinai was on a smoke because the
Lord was come down upon it in fire and the
smoke arose from it, as out of a furnace, and
all the mount was terrible. And the sound
of the trumpet grew by degrees, louder and
louder, and was drawn out to a greater
length; Moses spoke and God answered him.
And the Lord came down upon Mount Sinai,
in the very top of the Mount, and He called
Moses unto the top thereof.

And the Lord spoke all these words : " I
am the Lord thy God, who brought thee out,"
etc.

And the Lord, when He had ended these
words in Mount Sinai, gave to Moses two
stone Tables of testimony, written with the
Finger of God.—(Exodus xix., xxxi., 18).

> Note that in most cases the Command-
> ments are negative, *i.e.*, " Thou shalt
> not "; dwell on the *positive* side as
> much as possible.

Before teaching the Commandments make
children realise that they were given to Moses
and the Jews; we are strictly bound to keep
them, because when Our Lord came, He told
us to. But He requires much more of *us*,

than He did of the Jews—we have His example and the Sacraments to help us.

Compare with the Commandments.—Matt. xxii., 35-40 (quoted above), and Matt. v., 19-22, 33-48.

First Commandment

" Christ confirmed the Commandments in the New Law."

Our Lord said : " Do not think I am come to destroy the Law : I am not come to destroy but to fulfil."—(Matt. v., 17).

The account of the Presentation in the Temple might illustrate this—(Luke ii., 22-24). The fulfilment of the Law is mentioned three times in these three verses.

Our Lord built the New Law on the Old, and by so building He strengthened the foundation.

Q. 175.—Wording of the First Commandment.

"Any Graven thing."—Illustrate by the Golden Calf, " the likeness of a thing in the earth beneath."

"And the people seeing that Moses delayed to come down from the Mount, gathering together against Aaron, said : "Arise, make us gods that may go before us. For as to this Moses, the man that brought us out of the land of Egypt, we know not what has befallen him.   And Aaron said to them :

Take the golden earrings from the ears of your wives, and your sons and daughters, and bring them to me."

And when he had received them, he made of them a golden calf.

And they said :

"These are thy gods, O Israel, that have brought thee out of the land of Egypt."

And Aaron built an altar before it, and rising in the morning they offered holocausts and peace victims.

And the Lord spoke to Moses, saying : "Go, get thee down; thy people which thou hast brought out of the land of Egypt has sinned."

And Moses returned from the Mount carrying the two Tables of the testimony in his hand, written on both sides; and when he came nigh to the camp he saw the calf and the dances, and being very angry, he threw the Tables out of his hand and broke them at the foot of the Mount; and laying hold of the calf which they had made, he burnt it and beat it to powder.

And when the next day was come, Moses spoke to the people :

" You have sinned a very great sin; I will go up to the Lord if by any means I may be able to entreat Him for your crime."   And the Lord answered him: "He that sinned against Me, him will I strike out of My book."—(Exodus xxxii.).

N.B.—We are not tempted to commit idolatry, but when we prefer *anything* (*e.g.*, money) to God, we too make, as it were, a little golden calf to worship.

Q. 176.—By the First Commandment we are commanded to worship God by Faith, Hope, Charity and Religion.

"*Faith, Hope, Charity*" (see "The Little Ones," p. 103).

Religion.—Do not define. Illustrate by examples, *e.g.*, Abraham's sacrifice of his son Isaac to God was a great act of religion, because he showed that God was Master and Lord over everything.

After these things God said to Abraham:

"Take thy only begotten son Isaac, whom thou lovest, and go into the land of vision; and there thou shalt offer him for a holocaust upon one of the mountains which I will shew thee."

So Abraham rising up in the night, saddled his ass, and took with him two young men and Isaac his son, and when he had cut wood for the holocaust he went his way to the place which God had commanded him. And on the third day, lifting up his eyes, he saw the place afar off, and he said to his young men:

" Stay you here with the ass; I and the boy will go with speed as far as yonder, and after we have worshipped will return to you."

And he took the wood for the holocaust and laid it upon Isaac his son, and he himself carried in his hands fire and a sword. And as they two went on together, Isaac said to his father:

" My father."

And he answered : " What wilt thou son ?"

" Behold," saith he, " fire and sword; where is the victim for the holocaust ?"

And Abraham said : " God will provide Himself a victim for a holocaust, my son."

So they went on together. And they came to the place which God had shewn him, where he built an altar and laid the wood in order upon it; and when he had bound Isaac his son, he laid him on the altar upon the pile of wood. And he put forth his hand and took the sword to sacrifice his son.

And behold an Angel of the Lord from Heaven called to him saying: "Abraham, Abraham."

And he answered : " Here I am."

And he said to him :

" Lay not thy hand upon the boy, neither do thou anything to him; now I know that

thou fearest God and hast not spared thy
only son for My sake.''

Abraham lifted up his eyes and saw a ram
amongst the briars sticking fast by the horns,
which he took and offered for a holocaust
instead of his son. And the Angel of the Lord
called to Abraham a second time from
Heaven, saying : Because thou hast done this
thing and hast not spared thy only son for
my sake, I will bless thee, and I will multiply
thy seed as the stars of Heaven.—(Genesis
xxii.).

Qs. 177 and 178.—The sins against Faith
are :—False Religions ; Wilful Doubt ; Disbelief ; Denial of any Article of Faith ; Culp-
able Ignorance of the doctrines of the Church.

We expose ourselves to the danger of losing our Faith by neglecting our spiritual
duties, reading bad books, going to non-
Catholic schools, and taking part in the services or prayers of a false Religion.

A good way of getting the children to understand the above is to present the matter
in story form, *e.g.*, the story of Torquatus
in Wiseman's ''Fabiola'' would do, if
slightly adapted.

Torquatus, a young man living in Rome,
had been converted to Christianity by St.
Sebastian—therefore he was not *ignorant of
the doctrines of the Church.*

One day he met with some of his old companions, among whom was Fulvius, his evil angel, and at supper the conversation turned on the likelihood of a fresh persecution, breaking out in Rome. This led to abuse of the Christian Faith, till at last Torquatus could stand it no longer, and he broke in with : " It is a lie, a cursed lie."

" How do you know ?" sneered Fulvius.

" Because I am a Christian, and am ready to die for my Faith."

(There was, you see, *no denial of any article of Faith*, and evidently neither *doubt* nor *disbelief*, in Torquatus's mind ; *but* he was playing with fire. *Fulvius disbelieved*).

After supper, Fulvius got Torquatus to come to the gambling table and play at dice. This love of gambling had already got Torquatus into trouble, and he had promised Sebastian he would never play again. Fulvius led him on now to play until he had completely ruined him.

Then he had him in his power, and told him he was master of his character, his peace and his life ; that he must either go at once to the Christians with all the sins of that night on his soul, or to-morrow to the court, where he would be put to death as a Christian.

Torquatus said that he would do whatever

Fulvius wanted, but neither of these two things.

So Fulvius told him he was to go on pretending to be a Christian, but to act as traitor and deliver all his Christian friends into the hands of the Pagans.

And Torquatus agreed and did it.

He denied his Faith and betrayed his comrades because he made *friends with a bad man.* But that is not all the story; he began by *neglecting prayer, Mass, Holy Communion*—and that is the way all those who fall away from God begin.

Reading bad books is as bad as having bad friends.

Sins against Hope : Despair : Presumption.

Q. 179.—Judas is a good example of despair. Tell the whole story :—

1 His vocation; his love of Our Lord; the happy time he spent with Him. His first small unacknowledged theft; how little by little the habit grew; how he gave up fervent prayer.

2 His anger and bitterness against St. Mary Magdalen.—(Matt. xxvi., 14).

3 "*What* will you give me, and I will betray Him ?" For *any* sum he was willing to do the awful deed.

4 The Last Supper; the washing of the feet.

Probably his first Communion. "That which thou dost, do quickly."—(John xiii., 27). "And it was *night*." True night in Judas's soul.

5 The betrayal in the Garden. "*Friend, whereto art thou come . . .*"—(St. Matt. xxvi., 48).

6 After Our Lord's condemnation, Judas's repentance.—(Matt. xxvii.).

7 The final sin of despair. Make sure that the children understand why Judas's confession was a bad one:—

    (*a*) The accusation was full and complete.

    (*b*) So too the restitution of the ill-gotten money.

    (*c*) The sorrow was very great, *but* sorrow without *hope in God's mercy* is of no value.

This is the sin of Despair, we believe God will not pardon us.

Cf. Genesis iv., 13.—And Cain said to the Lord : "My iniquity is greater than that I may deserve pardon." This is sometimes true with man, but *never* with God. It is the devil's favourite lie, because he knows that if only he can get anyone to believe this lie on to the end, that soul is lost.

Speak strongly too about want of confidence—venial sins of distrust.

Presumption.—We are here below under a contract—a contract between God and us.

Give some simple examples, *e.g.*, your father says: "If you work hard, I will give you a present." We waste our time instead, therefore we have no right to the present.

> *Note.*—A very indulgent father might give us the present all the same, but we have lost our right to it.

Our contract with God is this:

God has promised us:

> *(a)* Heaven.
>
> *(b)* The means to get there.

We, in Baptism and since, have promised God that we will:

> *(a)* Do what He tells us.
>
> *(b)* Avoid what displeases Him.

Now, if we do not keep our side of the contract, we have no *right* to expect God to keep His. If we do, then we are *presuming* on God's mercy—this is an example of a sin of Presumption.

We do nothing to get to Heaven, but we rashly think that God will give it us all the same.

We rush into temptation, and we think God ought to work a miracle to keep us from sin.

Before we sin, we say to ourselves: " I will go to Confession and make it all right afterwards."

After a big sin, God may in His mercy, and very often does give us time and grace to repent, but He is not bound to. We have not kept our side of the contract and God therefore is not *bound* to His.

If, for instance, a man tries to swim through the Falls of Niagara, he is tempting God's Providence, *i.e.*, committing the sin of Presumption. He will in all probability be drowned. He has no right to expect a miracle —there is nothing to be gained by swimming the Falls, except vainglory.

Q. 182.—Sins against Religion: Dealing with the Devil.

Explain principle first.

God has put us in this world under certain conditions to which we must submit.

One of these conditions is that He has hidden the future from us.

Get children to tell what they know through Faith about the future, and lead them to see how insecure and uncertain all the rest is. People are sometimes very anxious to find out what is going to happen to them in this world and what *has* happened to those who are already dead.

God their Father has not told them, so they try to find out from God's greatest enemy, the devil.

The devil does not know the future, but he is very clever—has had a long experience, and often makes a sharp guess; besides, he does not in the least mind how many lies he tells, and people who are wicked enough to consult him are also fools enough to believe him.

Superstition.—Believing things have a power which they do not possess in themselves, and which the Church has not given them.

Spiritualists are those who are already in connection with the devil.

Charms are things done, used or worn, to bring about results which they cannot do naturally, *e.g.*, a horseshoe hung over a door to bring a blessing on the house.

Omens are certain events which are supposed to foretell good or evil, *e.g.*:

> "Happy is the bride which the sun shines on;
> Happy is the grave which the rain falls on."

> N.B.—Charms, omens, dreams, are harmless in themselves : the sin lies in trusting in them.

SIMONY.—See Acts viii., 9-25.

Q. 181.—The making of *images* is not forbidden by the First Commandment.

Attention may be drawn to the statues of

great men in public squares—the honour paid
to them—Primrose Day, in honour of
Beaconsfield—for years his statue was covered
with his favourite flower on the anniversary
of his death.

We honour Our Mother's picture—why?
Because we wish thus to honour the person
represented.   Apply this to the Crucifix and
images of Our Lady, the Angels and Saints.

We honour the Ambassador of a King,
also members of a Royal Family, but not as
much as the King himself, etc.

In the Church we have great Feasts and
lesser Feasts.

Q. 183.—*Sacrilege* is a sin against Religion,
because it is treating with great irreverence
either *holy persons*, *e.g.*, Priests, or *holy
things*, *e.g.*, a Crucifix, or *holy places*, *e.g.*,
a Church.

Second Commandment

Q. 188.—" To take His Name in vain "
means to pronounce His Name uselessly and
irreverently.

· **Q. 189.**—" Jehovah " : the Name given by
the Jews to God, but out of reverence and
fear, never pronounced by them.

Our Lord came, and the law of fear gave
place to the law of love.   We may and should

pronounce the Name of God, and bless it and love it.

(The Divine Praises might be taught).

The Holy Name of Jesus: (100 days indulgence: Plenary at death).

St. Paul says : " In the name of Jesus every knee shall bow."

Teach a reverent bowing of the head at the Holy Name.

It was imposed by command of the Angel : " Thou shalt call His Name Jesus " (Luke i., 31), and given at the Circumcision of Our Lord —Feast kept on January 1st (Luke ii., 21).

It is the omnipotent Name, before which the demons flee.

Ask for grace to pronounce It, as Our Lady and St. Joseph did at Nazareth.   Explain monogram I.H.S.

We must also speak with reverence of holy persons and things.

Holy Persons.—Those consecrated to God are holy.

" With all thy soul fear the Lord and reverence His priests " (Ecclus. vii., 31); above all our Holy Father the Pope.

Q. 190.—*Oaths.*—Calling God to witness to the truth of what we say.   A terrible sin to ask the God of all Truth to witness to a lie, or to call on Him unnecessarily.

E

Godwin, Earl of Kent, was suspected of being the murderer of King Edward's brother, Alfred. The King accused him of it one day at table. "O, King," he answered, "God be my witness : let this morsel be my last if I had any hand in that detestable crime." The morsel choked him, and he fell back dead.

Herod's oath was unjust as well as rash.— (Matt. xiv., 6-12).

A Vow is a solemn promise made to God to do something that is better than its contrary, *e.g.*, the vow taken by the Crusaders or by so many of our British Kings to visit Rome.

Jacob, son of Isaac, was once on a journey to Mesopotamia, and when he was come to a certain place and would rest in it after sunset, he took of the stones that lay there, and putting under his head, slept in the same place. And he saw in his sleep a ladder standing upon the earth and the top thereof touching heaven, and the Lord, leaning upon the ladder, saying to him : " I am the Lord God of Abraham thy father ; the land wherein thou sleepest I will give to thee and to thy seed, and in thee and thy seed all the tribes of the earth shall be blessed. And I will be thy Keeper whithersoever thou goest, and will bring thee back into this land ; neither will I leave thee till I have accomplished all that

I have said." And when Jacob awaked out of sleep he said : " Indeed the Lord is in this place and I knew it not." And trembling he said : " How terrible is this place ! This is no other but the House of God and the gate of Heaven."

And Jacob arising in the morning took the stone, which he had laid under his head, and set it up for a title, pouring oil upon the top of it. And *he made a vow*, saying : " If God shall be with me and shall keep me in the way by which I walk, and shall give me bread to eat and raiment to put on, and I shall return prosperously to my father's house, the Lord shall be my God, and of all things that Thou shalt give to me, I will offer tithes to Thee."

Example of a rash vow.—Jephte was a Ruler fighting under God, and he made a vow to the Lord, saying : " If Thou wilt deliver the children of Ammon into my hands, whosoever shall first come forth out of the doors of my house, and shall meet me when I return in peace from the children of Ammon, the same will I offer a holocaust to the Lord." And Jephte passed over to the children of Ammon to fight against them, and the Lord delivered them into his hands. And when Jephte returned to his house, his only daughter met him with timbrels and with dances : for he had no other children. And

when he saw her he rent his garments, and
said : "Alas ! my daughter, I have opened my
mouth to the Lord (meaning, I have vowed
to the Lord), and I can do no other thing."
And he did to her as he had vowed.

Jephte probably consecrated his daughter
to God in the service of the Tabernacle, but
his vow was rash and imprudent.

SINS AGAINST THE SECOND COMMANDMENT.

Q. 191. — *Blasphemy.*—A terrible sin :·
speaking with contempt of God or of His
Saints or His Church.

"And behold there went out the son of a
woman of Israel, and fell at words in the
camp with a man of Israel. And when he had
blasphemed the Name (of God) and had
cursed it, he was brought to Moses, and they
put him into prison till they might know what
the Lord would command.

And the Lord spoke to Moses, saying :
" Bring forth the blasphemer without the
camp, and let them that heard him put their
hands upon his head and let all the people
stone him. He that blasphemeth the Name
of the Lord, dying let him die."

And Moses spoke to the children of Israel,
and they brought forth him that had blasphemed without the camp, and they stoned
him.—(Lev. xxiv., 10-23).

Cursing.—Calling God's anger down on our neighbour or on any of God's creatures.

Asking God to work out our own evil will is a great dishonour to Him and a great sin against our neighbour. It may become a habit, and it is easily caught from others and, if found in us, easily copied by others.

Profane Words.—Speaking irreverently of holy things.

Our Lord's precept should be followed: " You have heard that it was said to them of old : Thou shalt not forswear thyself . . . but I say to you not to swear at all, but let your speech be yea, yea ; no, no ; and that which is over and above these is of evil."—(Matt. v., 33-37).

THIRD COMMANDMENT

Qs. 192 and 193.—" Six days shalt thou labour and shalt do all thy works, but on the seventh day is the Sabbath of the Lord thy God; thou shalt do no work on it, thou, nor thy son nor thy daughter, nor thy man-servant, nor thy maid-servant; for in six days the Lord made heaven and earth and the sea, and all things that are in them, and rested on the seventh day and sanctified it."—(Exodus xx., 9-11).

" Remember that thou also didst serve in Egypt, and the Lord thy God brought thee out from thence with a strong hand and a

stretched out arm.   Therefore hath He commanded thee that thou shouldst observe the
Sabbath day."—(Deut. v., 15).

Sabbath Day.—The Church changed the
day to Sunday, because of Easter and Pentecost.

On the Sunday of His Resurrection Our
Lord conquered sin and death for us : how
much greater a thing than delivering the Jews
from Egypt !

Qs. 194 and 230.—*Resting from Servile
Work.*—Heavy bodily work, usually done by
servants.   " Servus " means slave or servant.

"And it came to pass, when the children of
Israel were in the wilderness and had found
a man gathering sticks on the Sabbath day,
that they brought him to Moses and Aaron
and the whole multitude, and they put him
into prison, not knowing what they should
do with him.

And the Lord said to Moses : " Let that
man die, let all the multitude stone him
throughout the camp.   And when they had
brought him out, they stoned him and he died
as the Lord had commanded."

God had given the people a solemn warning :

" Keep you My Sabbath for it is holy unto
you; he that shall profane it shall be put to
death; he that shall do any work in it, his

soul shall perish out of the midst of his people.
Six days shall you do work; in the seventh
day is the Sabbath, the rest holy to the Lord.
Everyone that shall do any work on this day
shall die."

And the man who gathered the sticks knew
this.

Necessary servile work is allowed, but fore-
sight should reduce this to the minimum.

When many hundred years later, the
Jews had to fight against a strange King
Nicanor, this bad man purposed to set upon
them with all violence on the Sabbath day.
Many Jews had been taken captive, and had
to fight in his army, and they said to him:
"Do not act so fiercely and barbarously, but
give honour to the day that is sanctified, and
reverence Him that beholdeth all things."
That unhappy man asked if there were a
mighty One in heaven that had commanded
the Sabbath day to be kept. They answered:
"There is the living Lord Himself in
Heaven, the mighty One that commanded
the seventh day to be kept." Then he said:
"And I am mighty upon the earth, and I
command to take arms and to do the King's·
business." Nevertheless he prevailed not to
accomplish his design. Five and thirty·thou-
sand of his men were killed, and Nicanor was
slain in his armour.—(II. Machabees, xv.).

Q. 195.—Note the reason for abstaining from servile work. To give us time for prayer and for receiving the Sacraments, hearing sermons, reading good books : not primarily that we may have more time for amusements. Amusements are lawful and even desirable, if time for our spiritual duties is safeguarded. Giving scandal to the weak should be avoided.

Our Lord said : " The children are free. But that we may not scandalise them, you Peter and I, will do as they ask." See Matt. xvii., 23-26. (The stater in the fish's mouth, but the principle may be applied here).

God meant Sunday to be a day of rest and joy, a day to look forward to all through the week, and those who have not got the true faith keep it in quite the wrong spirit.

Earning money in any other honest way than by servile work is not forbidden on Sunday.

All public business transactions, *e.g.*, keeping shops open, are forbidden.

Q. 194.—Obligation of hearing Mass.

Qs. 229 and 232.—*Make the following clear.*

1 This is binding because of the Church's First Commandment. She explains to us how God wishes *us* to keep the Third Commandment of God.

When we obey the Church we obey God.

Like all the other Commandments of the Church, this one is binding under pain of grievous sin—that is to say, we grievously offend God, if, without any serious reason, we stay away from Mass on a Sunday or on one of the big Feast Days.

What do we mean by a serious reason?

Supposing we were told that if we called at a certain friend's door at 11 o'clock on Wednesday next, he would give us £1.

We should be careful to call—*but* we could not do so if we were really ill (a little headache or a little cold would not keep us away):

> If the weather was so bad that we could not get along the streets.
>
> If our mother was ill and really needed us.
>
> If our friend lived so far away that we could not walk the distance, and had no other means of going.

These would be serious reasons for not calling on our friend, although thereby we lost £1, and if there are such serious reasons as the above for not going to Mass on Sunday, we are not bound to go.

If we *can* we must, if we *can't*, God is not displeased. When we get older, even if our father and mother forbade us to go to Mass, we must manage to go all the same, for we must never displease God to please anyone, even our parents. You who are eight or nine years old, must already do your very best to get your father and mother to take you to Mass on Sundays, or at any rate to let you go alone : just as they let you go to school alone.

We must be present in the Church from the beginning to the end of Mass.

We must say our prayers during it, and if we do this we have done all we are *obliged* to do on Sunday.

Recommend   reception   of   Sacraments, Beads and Benediction. Also reading the life of a Saint.

Some of the children whose homes are not thoroughly Christian, will find even Sunday Mass a difficulty.

Speak to all of the infinite value of the Holy Sacrifice.

Tell them of the martyrs, who risked their lives even to hear one Mass, and joyfully went to a most cruel death as the result.

In pagan times, St. Saturninus—a priest under Diocletian—told the judge : " We assemble the people because we are Christians and are commanded to keep the Sunday holy." He was martyred for it.

St. Hilarion, a little boy, at the time of the same persecution, boldly owned he had been to Mass on Sunday : " I went there because

I wanted to, and no one forced me to go."
He was then carried off to prison and to
death, crying: "I thank Thee, my God, that
I may suffer something for Thee."

Blessed Margaret Clitheroe was crushed to
death between two huge stones because she
had sheltered priests in London, and had
made it possible for them to say Mass at night
in her house—a Mass which she and her perse-
cuted fellow-Catholics heard at the risk of
their lives. (Martyred on Good Friday,
March 25, 1586. Called "the Pearl of
York." Countless examples might be cited).

Remind the children that they are the children of Martyrs.

THE FOURTH COMMANDMENT

Qs. 196 and 197.—The best place to learn
all about the Fourth Commandment is
Nazareth.

Develope the following points or others:—

    1 Our Lord was God of Heaven and
      Earth.

    2 Our Lady was His Mother: St. Joseph
      His Foster Father.

    3 Our Lord—Obeyed them:

            Reverenced them.
            Loved them.
            Worked hard for them.

Was ever patient and kind.
Did *their* will rather than
His own.

Practical applications.

Q. 204.—*Secret Societies are forbidden by the Church.*

Children of nine years old can hardly be expected fully to understand this.

Teach very simply:

(a) That God has willed us in this world to be obedient to—(i.) the Church; (ii.) those who govern our country.

(b) That there always have been and are now, men who refuse this obedience, and who meet together to do harm either to the Church or to those who govern the country.

(c) They know if they are found out they will be punished, so they meet together in secret.

(d) The Church forbids us to have anything to do with such meetings.

Freemasons, in this country, do not plot against the Church or State, all the same, a Catholic cannot join them, as it would be joining a *Secret* Society.

St. Paul warns us that everyone must be obedient to those above them—if they resist *them*, they resist God, and *that* resistance will purchase Hell for them.

Fifth Commandment

Q. 205.—Note that the Commandment is not : " Thou shalt not kill thy neighbour," but—" Thou shalt not kill." Therefore we ourselves are included; and it is a dreadful sin of murder, called *suicide*, for anyone to take his own life.

Our lives belong to God, and therefore to take a life is a grievous sin against Him.

We are here to save our soul, and by such an act, we should throw it into Hell.

We are here to do good to others, so we should sin against our neighbour too.

Q. 207.—*Anger.*—Note that it may be just (*i.e.*, no sin) or unjust. Our Lord "looked on the Sadducees and Pharisees with *anger*," and He drove the buyers and sellers out of the Temple in *anger*.

Just Anger :

    i. Must have a just cause;

    ii. Must be strictly under our control;

    iii. Must be in proportion to the offence.

Q. 208.—*Scandal :* A stumbling block.

Take a familiar example of something tripping you up and causing you to fall.

    i. Eve was a scandal to Adam.

    ii. She ate the fruit, therefore she sinned.

    iii. She went to Adam with the apple in her hand, told him it was a beauti-

ful fruit, and persuaded him to eat
it with her : she sinned again : the
sin of scandal.

1 Our Lord was one day telling the Apostles
all about Good Friday, which was draw-
ing very near, and St. Peter, who could
not bear to think of all He would have
to suffer, began to try to persuade Him
not to endure it all.

Our Lord rebuked him sharply—told him
that was the devil's work to try to prevent
others from doing God's Will. That is what
we must answer when others tempt us to sin.

2 Indirect scandal or bad example.

Take any familiar example : e.g., speaking
disrespectfully to parents, before younger
brothers and sisters.

SIXTH, NINTH AND TENTH COMMANDMENTS
Qs. 209=213, 223=227.

1 Put a picture of Our Lady before the class.

2 Explain that our bodies are temples of the
Holy Ghost, i.e., God dwells in them.
The Tabernacle on the altar is the holiest
part of the Church, because God dwells
there ; so too our hearts, into which
Jesus so often comes, must always be
holy and kept for Him.

3 So in all our actions, all our words and
looks, we must be modest and holy. Re-

member Our Blessed Lady—Mother most pure—and try to be like Her.

4 When we see pictures or plays, etc., that are wicked and immodest, we must turn away our eyes, because these bad things might stain our souls. So too, when we hear bad words or find out that a book we are reading is bad, we must turn away at once. We cannot touch pitch and not be defiled.

Q. 225.—*What must we do to avoid all such evil?* We must practice mortification in food and drink; we must work; have nothing to do with wicked people, and above all—we must *pray*.

Teach the children to say every night, before getting into bed, three Hail Maries in honour of Our Lady's Immaculate Conception.

Refer to some familiar hymn to Our Lady, which dwells on her purity.

Q. 224.—*Sins of Thought.*—We know that there are four ways in which we may sin, and *thought* is one of them.

We can sin by thought:

    i. By thinking with pleasure of what displeases God. If God hates it, I must hate it too.

    ii. By *wishing to do* what I know displeases God.

    iii. By making up my mind that I *will* do it.

The children will easily see that this is the worst.

1 Supposing a boy or girl is looking in at a shop window. They see, for instance, a pretty necklace, or a fine cricket bat. They think to themselves: "How I should like that!" Here there is no sin at all.

2 "I wish I could get it! How could I manage it? If I stole it, I might be caught. . . . Still there is no one looking," etc.

    [Here they are playing with temptation, and there may be venial sin. They should have turned away at: "How could I manage it?"]

3 "I'll get it if I can . . . not now, but to-night when it is dark," etc.

    [This is a sin of thought, and if the thing in question is valuable, it is a grievous one.]

SEVENTH COMMANDMENT

Q. 214.—Be careful not to give many suggestive examples with regard to the sin of theft, thereby putting ideas into the children's heads, which might easily turn into temptation.

i. A man is a thief if he take away or keep what is not his.

ii. He is a robber if he takes it away openly or by force.

iii. He is a cheat if he pretends to do the just thing, and in reality takes away what is not his.

Judas was both a thief and a cheat.

The wretched Barabbas whom the Jews preferred to Our Lord was a robber.

The two who were crucified with Him had been thieves.

Q. 216.—There are many ways of stealing :

To take full wages when we have only earned a part.

Not to pay our debts.

To use false weights and measures when selling.

To buy or sell what we know has been stolen.

Deliberately to spoil or waste what does not belong to us.

To keep things. we have found or borrowed.

If in any of these ways a person does another serious harm, it is a grievous sin, and God will not forgive him unless he confesses it, and does what the priest tells him, about giving the thing back.

F

If it is a little thing he must be sorry, and he ought to try to give it back.

God made known to Josue, who on the death of Moses became leader of the people of Israel, that a certain man called Achan had stolen what belonged to the treasures of the Lord.

"And Josue said to Achan : My son, give glory to the Lord God of Israel, and confess and tell me what thou hast done, hide it not."

And Achan answered Josue and said to him :

"Indeed I have sinned against the Lord, the God of Israel, and thus have I done. For I saw among the spoils a scarlet garment exceedingly good, and two hundred sicles of silver, and a golden rule of fifty sicles; and I coveted them, and I took them away and hid them in the ground in the midst of my tent, and the silver I covered with the earth that I dug up."

Josue therefore sent ministers, who running to his tent, found all hidden in the same place, together with the silver. And taking them away out of the tent, they brought them to Josue, and to all the children of Israel, and threw them down before the Lord. Then Josue and all Israel with him, took Achan and the silver, and the garments and the golden rule, his sons also and his daughters, his oxen and asses and sheep, the tent also and all the goods, and brought them to the valley of Achor. And all Israel stoned him, and all things that were his were consumed in fire.—(Josue vii., 19-26).

Get children to see that if a boy or girl becomes a thief they do so by little and little. They begin by taking little things, *e.g.*, pennies to get to the pictures; then by degrees the habit grows.

Eighth Commandment

Q. 219.—Our Lord once told His Apostles that they would give testimony of Him, *because they had been with Him* from the beginning.

He meant that when speaking to others of what He had said and done, they would be able to add: "We know it is true because we were there at the time. We saw it with our own eyes and heard it with our own ears."

In the same way, when St. Luke wanted to write an account of the Birth and Childhood of Our Lord, Our Lady gave testimony: She could bear witness better than anyone else. She would testify to the truth of every fact.

If ever we have to give testimony against our neighbour, we must be very careful to state what we really know to be facts, giving things certain as certain, and doubtful as doubtful, etc., otherwise we should " bear false witness," and if the matter is serious, this is a grievous sin.

Those who give testimony or bear witness in a Court of Justice are on oath; and therefore to say what is not true would be taking God's Name in vain, and breaking the Second as well as the Eighth Commandment.

Q. 220.—Rash Judgment.—Distinguish between Rash Suspicion and Rash Judgment. Both are sins against Charity : in the former we wonder and guess; in the latter we make up our mind about the thing in question.

If we do this without sufficient reason, we injure our neighbour by keeping from him what he has a right to—our good opinion. If he has no right to it, then there is no sin.

At the Last Supper *no* one suspected Judas. Each feared for himself.—(John xiii., 21-26).

St. Paul tells us we are to think no evil but believe all things, hope all things (I. Cor., xiii.), and he means believe and hope all good of everybody—as long as you possibly can.

When we come to die Our Lord will judge us, as severely or as mercifully as we have judged others. He promised us this, and He added that the measure of our mercy and kindness to others is the measure of His mercy and kindness to us.—(Matt. vii., 1, 2).

Lies.—Saying what we know to be false in order to deceive—speaking against our own thought. We may do it in jest,* or because we want some good, or hope to avoid some evil; or worst of all, a lie may be told expressly to do harm to other people, which is a very wicked thing to do.

Give story of Ananias and Saphira.—(Acts v., 1-11).

> *Note.*—Explain that in the Early Church the Christians had all things in common, and Ananias and Saphira had agreed to this, though they were quite free not to (see v., 4), therefore they cheated : they acted a lie first, and then they told one.

Most lies are told through fear of some kind of blame, or pain or punishment. We must pray to be brave, and to remember at the right time that the punishment of God for the lie will be far worse than the punishment of man for the fault, even if, through our frankness in speaking the truth, we do not escape the latter.

Q. 221.—Calumny.—Saying what we know to be false against our neighbour : a sin against truth and against charity.

Q. 222.—Those who commit it are bound to give back what they have taken away, *i.e.*,

---

* We want to amuse ourselves, generally at someone else's expense.

their neighbour's good name—just as a thief
would be bound to give back the purse he had
stolen; the good name is the more valuable
of the two.

Detraction.—Saying true but unkind things
of our neighbour—making known his secret
faults. This harm cannot be undone because
what was said is true; all that can be done is
to make up by kind words and deeds for the
injury done. Both Calumny and Detraction
are grievous sins if the injury done is serious.

Backbiting.—This means talking of the
known faults of our neighbour behind his
back.

Tale-bearing.—Carrying tales of our neighbour backwards and forwards, with no result
beyond the detestable one of setting one person against another.

St. James the Apostle tells us that we shall
be perfect if we never sin with our tongue.
He reminds us how, by putting a bit into a
horse's mouth, we can lead him where we
will; so too, if we bridle our tongue, we shall
be able to serve God more faithfully than the
horse serves us.

Again he says, great ships driven by strong
winds are nevertheless turned by a small
helm, so too our tongues, though small, can
do great things for good or evil.

When speaking of a tongue that tells lies,

talks against its neighbour and bears false witness, he calls it: "a fire—a world of iniquity—being set on fire by hell."—(James iii.).

Speak of the value of kind words.

THE COMMANDMENTS OF THE CHURCH

Q. 223.—"He that heareth You, heareth Me; and he that despiseth You, despiseth Me."

This means: "When the Church speaks to you, I, the Man-God, speak; if you disobey the Church, you disobey Me."

CHIEF COMMANDMENTS of the Church: there are many others—these six we have to know by heart:

Q. 231.—Holidays of Obligation.—The dates of these should be known, and enough said about each to leave a picture in the child's mind.

As each Feast occurs some instruction will probably be given on it in school, so that by degrees the whole Liturgical Year will become a living reality in the children's lives.

Q. 240.—The Third Commandment of the Church bids us go to Confession at least once a year, and children are bound to this as soon as they "come to the use of reason, so as to be capable of mortal sin."

Once we understand what it means to do something very wrong, we *could* of course do it, if we were very wicked and made up our minds to turn our back on God and lose Heaven and go to Hell instead. But if only we say our prayers and go to Holy Communion we shall never do such terrible things. We must " use our reason," which tells us that sin is the worst evil that can come to us.

Q. 247.—Sixth Commandment of the Church—"Not to solemnise marriage at forbidden times." It is not allowed during the forbidden times, to have the Nuptial Mass or Blessing, or any festivities. (The Bishop may give permission in special cases). People can have the Sacrament if they want to.

All Catholics must be very careful to do what the Church tells them about marriage. They cannot get married at all without a priest.

SECTION III.

Faith and the Ninth Article of the Creed.

Q. 9.—*Faith.*—Distinguish between believing a fact and believing in a Person. The events of Our Lord's Life are historical facts : that He is God is a Mystery, which Faith enables us to believe.

We could believe without the virtue of Faith that He was born at Bethlehem—just as we believe that Mary Stuart was beheaded at Fotheringay, though no one living saw the execution.

What we must pray to God for is Faith in Him—in the all-powerful and all-good God—Who is Our Father, Who does everything for us . . . and Faith in His Son, Jesus Christ Our Lord, Who died for each one of us, and Who would do anything in the wide world for us.

Example of Faith:

St. Thomas : "My Lord and my God!"

St. Peter : " Lord save me or I perish !"
etc.

When God sends us what we do not like and
do not understand, then is the time, above all
others, to show our Faith; also when we are
tempted to sin and we lean on God and so
resist.

Our God Whom we believe in so firmly,
and Who is our very good Father, has told
us many things about Himself and about His
works to help us to get to Heaven.   And we
learn all of it eagerly and gladly, and we believe it with all our heart and mind.

Some of it He told us when He was on
earth.

Q. 11.—A King might, if he chose, say to
his people : "I am going away for a very long
time; I leave you my Minister—look to him—
everything he says I say too; if you believe
him, you believe me; if you obey him you
obey me—he knows all I want you to know,
and I have taught him so well, that he cannot
make a mistake.

(Apply to the Church).

This Minister would bear witness to his
King, and the King would back him up.   He
would speak in the King's name, as if he
himself were King, because the King had told
him to—he would have the King's authority.

Q. 12.—Get the children to say the Creed,

inserting the words : " I believe," before each
article.

Sum up, at the end, *why* we believe it.

NINTH ARTICLE OF THE CREED.

Q. 84.—Get the children to understand the
difference between a crowd and a body of
men, *i.e.*, in a general way, what is meant by
organization.

Take as an example, a nation :

A King is the Head if it is a Kingdom,
e.g., Great Britain.

A President, if it is a Republic, *e.g.*,
America :

He governs through his Ministers,
Parliament or Senate, etc.

The People are the governed.

The Body, *i.e.*, the Nation, was
founded so many hundred years
ago.

Q. 85.—Nineteen hundred years ago God
sent His Son to found a great Body, which,
some day, is to include the whole world.
(There shall be one fold).

The Head is Jesus Christ.

He governs through the Pope and
Bishops and Priests.

His People, the Faithful, are the
governed.

The Faithful are you and I, and all those

who believe in Him ; a beautiful name, which
we must deserve till death.

[A B.B. sketch would obviously help
here; also sketch of rock in stormy sea,
and Church (with light) on summit.
Text: " Thou art Peter," etc., printed
underneath.]

Q. 88.—It is an historical fact that St.
Peter and all his successors have been Bishops
of Rome.

A list something like the following on B.B.,
to be read only, might impress the children
with the glorious line of Sovereign Pontiffs :—

St. Peter (martyred about A.D. 67).
St. Linus.
St. Anacletus.
St. Clement.
40 others in succession.
St. Leo I. (A.D. 440).
18 others in succession.
St. Gregory I.
53 others in succession.
St. Pascal I. (A.D. 817).
58 others in succession.
St. Gregory VII. (1073).
35 others in succession.
Boniface VIII. (A.D. 1294).
29 others in succession.
Paul III. (1534).
24 others in succession.

Benedict XIII.
10 others in succession.
Pius IX. (1878).
Leo XIII. (1903).
Pius X. (1914).
Benedict XIV. (1922).

Pius XI. is the 261st Pope, in unbroken succession, from St. Peter.

Vicar means one who is appointed by another to act in his name.

Q. 90.—*Spiritual Father* means Father of our souls—they are spirits.

Q. 91.—*Shepherd, Sheep, Flock, Lambs*— all figures of speech used by Our Lord Himself, and therefore very dear to us : always used when speaking of the Church.

Recall the scene by the Lake.—(St. John xxi., 15-18).

Q. 93.—*Infallibility.*—It stands to reason that Christ's Church must be *infallible.* If She *could* make a mistake, She would have done so long ago, because no man without God's special help can always be right; but this would mean that Our Lord Himself could teach us what is false, and oblige us to believe it. This is of course impossible, therefore Our Lord made it impossible for the Church to go wrong.

Infallibility means that when the Church

teaches us what to believe and what to do, She cannot make a mistake.

Q. 94.—*Marks of the Church.* A forester once said to his woodcutter : " Go and cut down all the trees in that plantation except one." He pointed in the direction of the wood. The woodcutter said : "Sir, there are many trees in that plantation. Which is the only one I am not to cut down ?" " You cannot make a mistake," said the forester, " it is the only tree that has these four marks :— 1. It is the only tree whose trunk is not split; 2. It bears more fruit than any other tree in the whole plantation ; 3. It grows in every part of the country ; 4. It is the oldest tree in the wood—it was planted before any of the others." The woodcutter went to the wood, and after careful examination he found there was only one tree that had all these four marks, and so he cut down all the others, and left that one standing alone as the forester had said.

Q. 95.—*The Church is One.*—Every Catholic believes the same thing : all hear Mass and go to Confession and Communion, and are all obedient to the Pope.

Q. 96.—*Holy.*—All that the Church teaches us is holy. She gives us what makes us holy : the Holy Mass, the Sacraments, etc., and She has sent to Heaven many thousands of Saints.

Q. 97.—*Catholic.*—The Church is catholic, or universal, because She remains the same since Our Lord founded Her. She teaches all men. She, like the Ark in which Noe and his family were saved, is the one Church in which all who will, can be saved.

Q. 99.—*Apostolic.*—Whatever the Apostles taught and wrote the Church teaches us. All Her Priests and Bishops get their power to offer sacrifice and give the Sacraments, and their right to do so, from the direct successors of the Apostles.

Q. 100.—*The Church is our Infallible Guide.*—The signpost guides to the direction of the town; the Polar Star points to the North; the Sanctuary Lamp points to where the Blessed Sacrament is, etc.

Faith and Morals.—" Faith and Morals " means what we have to believe and what we are to do.

The Communion of Saints.

Q. 102.—Draw the frame of a triptych on the B.B. Fasten three pictures into the frames :—

    i. Of Our Lady. Print underneath— " Mary, Gate of Heaven, intercede for the suffering souls in Purgatory."

    ii. Of the Crucifixion or of the priest

saying **Mass.**   Write   underneath—
" Earth."

iii. Of Our Lord or of the Sacred Heart
in   glory.   Write   underneath—
" Heaven."

Explain how these three pictures represent
the three great divisions of the Church's children (militant, suffering and triumphant),
and obtain reasons for these names.

All these *one* Church ; all united, and united
so closely that we speak of " Communion " of
all the Faithful, never mind which division
they belong to—the " Communion of Saints."

Develop these two truths :—

i. The Holy Mass brings all three divisions
together before the Throne of God.

ii. Grace is the great linking bond between
them.

PURGATORY.
Q. 106.

1 The *mercy* of temporal punishment : e.g.,—
a great criminal is condemned to death :
his sentence is changed to some months
imprisonment.

A man dies—quite unfit to appear in the
Courts of Heaven. He would die of shame,
so to speak, if St. Peter brought him in ; but
he loves God and he is saved. He gladly goes
to Purgatory that he may mend the beauti-

ful robe he got in Baptism, and which he has since torn and stained.

2 Why souls go to Purgatory.

Distinguish between guilt and punishment. Guilt is the responsibility of a wicked deed. We have to answer to God for all our deeds, and if they are bad He is displeased with us, and He says we are *guilty*. Then comes real sorrow, and we ask God's pardon whilst we are still on earth. God forgives us, and so our guilt passes away never to return. But punishment remains, because God has decreed that every sin shall be punished either on earth, or if the punishment is not completed at death, then in Purgatory.

3 Suffering.

The Church teaches that the suffering in Purgatory is greater than anything we can feel in this world. We should remember this when we are tempted to sin; and we should remember it too for the sake of the Holy Souls whom we can help by our prayers.

Supposing you were shut up in a little, dark room in great pain for a long, long time. You knew your mother was just outside— only one wall between you and her—and that she would stop the pain the moment you got to her. But you could neither see nor hear her, and you remained locked up. You could not make a hole through the wall. You would

G

suffer very much, and your longing to get to
your mother would get worse every day; but
it would be as nothing compared with the
longing of the Holy Souls to see God. Now,
by our prayers, we can, as it were, make a
hole in the wall of their prison cell and let
them out.

Q. 300.

Indulgences.

The Treasury of the Church is made up of
Her riches, just as the treasury of the nation
is made up of the riches of that nation. The
riches of the Church, the money with which
She purchases Heaven for Her children, are
the merits of Our Blessed Lord, Our Lady,
and the extra merits of the Saints.

Merit is the reward due through God's promise for a good work done by a soul in grace.

The Church draws from Her Treasury to
help Her faithful children on earth and in
Purgatory, and She gives us the right to draw
from it too, if we do what She tells us. That
is what is meant by gaining an Indulgence.

She generally tells us to go to Confession
once a fortnight, to receive Holy Communion,
and to pray for the Pope. Also to say certain prayers to which She " has attached an
Indulgence."

Explain terms " Plenary " and " Partial."
Also such expressions as " Seven Years and

Seven Quarantines," etc. (refer to ancient canonical penances); teach the "Prayer before a Crucifix" after Holy Communion, and make it clear that a state of grace is necessary for the gaining of any Indulgence— Plenary or Partial.

GRACE—HABITUAL AND ACTUAL.

Q. 139.—Give the Parable of the Wedding Garment.—(Matt. xxii. 2-14).

The man had been entirely to blame, because wedding garments used to hang near the door of the Feast Chamber, for the use of those who had not got one; he had only to give himself the trouble to take one down and put it on.

Habitual Grace is like the Wedding Garment—it clothes our soul entirely, and is so beautiful that God loves the soul that is clothed with it. It is pure, and God loves purity; it is bright, and reflects God. It makes the soul the dwelling-place of the Holy Ghost on earth and fit for Heaven, just as the wedding garment would have made the man fit for the Feast. He was without it, and therefore was cast into the exterior darkness, and that is exactly what happens to a soul who at death is without Habitual Grace.

Note.—It is most important to make the children understand that Sanctifying or

Habitual Grace gives *a new life* to the soul—a *super*-natural life, so that with it, the soul can do what otherwise would be absolutely impossible. Slow and careful teaching is needed of this all-important matter, but it is well worth while to go on, till it is thoroughly grasped.

The following might be taught, and put on B.B. :—

VEGETABLE LIFE—*e.g.*, a cabbage :
> It feeds.
> It grows.
> It produces other cabbages.

ANIMAL LIFE—*e.g.*, a cow. Besides the above—
> It moves.
> It has five senses.
> It feels pain, pleasure, etc.

REASONABLE LIFE—Man. He can do all the above, and—
> He thinks.
> He chooses for himself.

Unlike the cow, he has free-will : he can't be forced to choose, and he knows *why* he chooses.

This reasonable life is man's *natural* life, and he will *never* lose it, whether the man be lost or saved.

That is what we mean when we say our soul

is immortal; we are talking of our natural, reasonable life. This natural life will never get the soul to Heaven, nor even one little step on the road there.

Go back to the cabbage for a moment:

Ask the cabbage to work a sum in arithmetic.

What must be given to the cabbage before it can do that?

A reasonable life, which will make it possible for the cabbage to think; otherwise it will never get one tiny step nearer to doing the sum.

The same with the natural life of the soul and its efforts to get to God.

When God made animals He gave them a higher life than the one He gave vegetables; and as He wants our souls close to Himself, He pours a higher life than the reasonable one into our souls. And just as the higher life of the animals makes it possible for them to do what the vegetables cannot, so this higher life which God gives us in Baptism, makes it possible for us to believe in Him, hope in Him, love Him, serve Him, and so get to see Him face to face in Heaven.

All this is quite as impossible for the soul without Habitual Grace (which is the name given to this higher life of the soul), as it is for the cabbage to do the arithmetic sum.

This is the life we have to take so much care of.

Our bodily life, which we and the animals both have, is very precious to us, because as long as our body and soul are united together on earth, we can merit Heaven and work for God, and also because we all fear death. Our reasonable life cannot be destroyed—mortal sin and that alone can and does destroy this highest and most beautiful life which we call Habitual or Sanctifying Grace, and which is certain to get us to Heaven if we take care of it.

On B.B.—

NATURAL LIFE OF THE BODY : destroyed by death.

NATURAL LIFE OF THE SOUL : can never be destroyed.

SUPERNATURAL LIFE OF THE SOUL (Habitual Grace) : destroyed by mortal sin only.

Therefore mortal sin is quite clearly the greatest of all evils.

Some animals have a stronger bodily life than others; so have some men a stronger bodily life and a stronger reasonable life than others.

The supernatural life, called grace, which God has given to our souls may also grow stronger :

(a) By receiving the Sacraments.

(b) By praying.

(c) By every good act we do for God, just as bodily exercise makes the body grow strong, so too serving God makes the supernatural life of the soul (Habitual Grace) grow strong.

ACTUAL GRACE.

The word " Grace " means a gift, and besides this Habitual Grace, which we get in Baptism, and which clothes our soul, God gives us what are called *"Actual* Graces," which help us to do our *actions* well.

They are special helps, giving us light and strength to avoid what is wrong, and to do what God wants.

When Our Lord forgave St. Mary Magdalen and other poor sinners their sins, He clothed their souls with Habitual Grace, so that they became pleasing to Him and fit for Heaven.

When He said : " Go, and sin no more," this was a promise that He would give them actual graces or helps, so that when temptation came, they would have strength to resist and do His Will.

Examples of Actual Grace:

The Prodigal Son said : "I will arise and go to my father, and say to him : Father, I have sinned against Heaven and before thee."

A poor sinner cannot say that to God unless God helps him to see that he has done wrong and to be sorry, and that help is an "Actual Grace."

The Father here represents God : the Son, any poor sinner. The Father's forgiveness was complete—*i.e.*, He gave him back his supernatural life or Habitual Grace which he had lost, and which is typified by the "first robe," which the Father ordered to be put upon the poor prodigal.

When Our Lord cured the lunatic boy, He said to his father who had begged so earnestly for the cure, that He would hear his prayer if only he believed. The father answered : "I do believe Lord : help Thou my unbelief."

Our Lord had given him an actual grace, which helped him to make this beautiful answer, and the man by his prayer asked for still more grace.—(St. Mark ix., 16-26).

When St. Peter said to Our Lord : "Thou art Christ, the Son of the Living God," he had received an actual grace, which enabled him to make his act of Faith. "The Father had revealed it to him "; an Actual Grace of Light for his mind.—(Matt. xvi., 13-19).

A certain woman who had committed a great sin was brought to Our Lord ; the Jews wanted to stone her, but Our Lord saved her,

and then added: "Neither will I condemn
thee: go and now sin no more."

The children ought to be able to say that
Our Lord gave her back "Habitual Grace."

The graces given to St. Paul (see Acts ix.,
1-20) might be pointed out by the children,
and the distinction between Habitual and
Actual Grace obtained.

What Our Lord did when He was on earth
He does still in the Confessional.

When God gives us an Actual Grace we
must use it: otherwise it will not do us any
good, and if we neglect it deliberately, we
are very ungrateful.

Go through the children's day with them,
and point out some of the many actual graces
they every day receive.

Comment on the following:

"Behold I stand at the door and knock;
if any man shall hear My voice and open to
Me the door, I will come into him and sup
with him and he with Me."—(Apoc. iii., 20).

"I can do all things in him who strength-
eneth Me."—(Philip. iv., 13).

PRAYER.

We have seen something of our need of
Grace, and one great means of strengthening
our Supernatural Life (Habitual Grace), and
of obtaining Actual Graces, is Prayer.

Q. 141.—"Prayer is the raising up of the mind and heart to God."

Prayer means turning our whole selves to God, in the same kind of way as we turn towards a great friend who comes to greet us.

Prayer means talking to God as we do to this great friend, or to our father and mother.

Prayer means thinking of God with love, just as we do of those on earth, whom we love and whom we cannot see.

Prayer means a glance towards Heaven, where God, Our Lord, Our Lady and the Saints are.

Therefore we see that no words we have learnt by heart are necessary—we can use our own; indeed, no words at all are needed, as the thought of our mind and the love of our heart, if given to God, are Prayer.

e.g.—We are very cold in winter-time, and we give a glance of our mind at the Crib and think : "Never mind : Our Lord bore the cold for me." That is Prayer.

We have a warm thought for the last Communion we have made. That is Prayer.

We cannot get our work done, and we give a look towards Our Lord for help. That is Prayer.

We are tempted to do wrong, and we, as it were, clutch hold of Our Lord's Hand to prevent ourselves falling. That is Prayer.

1 We are bound to pray, because God Our
   Lord has commanded it :—
   " Watch ye and pray that ye enter not into
     temptation."—(Matt. xxvi., 41).
   "Ask and you shall receive; seek and you
     shall find ; knock and it shall be opened
     unto you."—(John xvi., 23-27).
   " We ought always to pray and not to
     faint."—(Luke xviii., 1).
   " Everyone that asketh receiveth, and he
     that seeketh findeth, and to him that
     knocketh, it shall be opened."—(Matt.
     vii., 8).
   " Thus therefore shall you pray : Our
     Father," etc.—(Matt. vi., 9-13).

2 We are bound to pray, because only thus
   can we get grace sufficient to get us to
   Heaven.

Prayer is the Key to Heaven.

Never yet was a soul lost except through
neglect of prayer. Lay stress on this great
truth.

KINDS OF PRAYER.

Vocal Prayer : in this we use our voice in
prayers written as a rule by others, and make
them our own, repeating the same words.
This kind of prayer is very good—many vocal
prayers are the Church's own—*e.g.*, the

prayers said by the priest at Mass—the Psalms, the Our Father, the Hail Mary, etc.

Many others the Church has approved of for our use, and has attached Indulgences to —*e.g.*, The Rosary—the Angelus—the Divine Praises—Our Lady's Litany—the Memorare —the Acts of Faith, Hope and Charity.

These prayers contain all the chief things which we Catholics ought to say to God daily, or at any rate, frequently.

MENTAL PRAYER.

This might also be called wordless prayer, in which, as in vocal prayer, our minds and hearts are fixed on God, but in which, without any set words, we adore Him—praise, thank, love—ask for all we want—or think over quietly what He is, and what He has done for the world and for us. This is what the poor man of Ars did, who, when St. John Baptiste Vianney asked him what he said to Our Lord in the long visits he every day paid Him, answered: "I say nothing to Him: I look at Him and He looks at me."

Sometimes for this kind of prayer it is a help to picture to ourselves some scene from the Gospels, or recall any real picture we are fond of. This fixes our mind and makes it easier to pray. For instance, we remember how, when Our Lord was on earth, a leper

came and adored Him, saying: "Lord, if
Thou wilt, Thou canst make me clean," and
Jesus, stretching forth His Hand, touched
him, saying: "I will, be thou made clean."—
(Luke v., 12, 13).

We might use those two verses when we
pay a visit to the Blessed Sacrament, or to
prepare or thank for Holy Communion or
Confession.

We see Our Lord standing in the street
surrounded by a crowd, who all draw back as
they see the poor leper coming nearer. We
ask Him that we may never draw back when
there is something hard or disagreeable to do
for Him. We tell Him we want to keep close
to His side. Then we see the leper kneel
down : we kneel with him, for we know that
Jesus is God. We hear the leper's prayer and
we join in it, asking to be cleansed from sin.
"Lord, if Thou wilt, Thou canst." That is
a prayer which we can always say, for it is
always true : whatever our need, if He wills,
He can help us. There is nothing He cannot
do if He wills : so we make our act of Faith
and also of trust, that whatever is good for
us, that He wills. Then we see Him stretching forth His Hand : that same Hand that
was soon to be pierced by a big nail; it was
the Hand Our Lady loved so well—the Hand
that is so often raised to bless me, and which

when I come to die, will be stretched out to welcome me.

And now I see it touching the poor leper, and repeating his words: "I will, be thou made clean." And I watch the wonderful change that takes place and I praise Our Lord Who is so strong. I try to get closer to His side, even than the leper was.

Or we might take the fourth chapter of St. Mark, and see how Our Lord calls Himself the Sower of Seed.

I ask Him to sow some seeds in my heart, especially what I want most to grow there; kindness, or truth, or whatever it is. I speak too of my little patch of weeds, and ask Him to get rid of them for me.

And also that He may turn my heart into very good ground, so that He may be able to gather much fruit from it. I beg Him not to let the thorns grow there, and never to let it become stony ground, etc.

Note.—The Gospel is the best of Prayer Books, but the children will not use it as such without training and help. It is suggested that many incidents in Our Lord's Life be taught in this way, so that they may furnish matter for prayer.

Dispositions for Prayer.

It is hard to pray and get no answer, but

we must remember that God *always* sends us an answer if we pray in the right way and for the right things.

You would not give your little baby brother a sharp knife to play with, however much he cried for it.

If God sees that what we are asking for will do us harm, of course He will not give it; we are bound to make this act of trust with regard to prayer. And as He knows best, we always pray in submission to His Will.

Let us study some of the prayers Our Lord answered immediately, when He was on earth, and which He therefore evidently liked.

1 THE SYROPHENICIAN WOMAN.—(St. Matt. xv., 22-30).

   Note.—i. Humility : She fell down at His Feet.

   ii. Faith : She adored Him.

   iii. Perseverance : He is silent : she goes on praying. He compares her to the dogs; she answers with another humble prayer.

Result : Our Lord not only answers her prayer, but praises her Faith.

2 THE STILLING OF THE TEMPEST.—(Mark iv., 36-40).

Note that though Our Lord answered this

prayer, He found fault with it.   What was wrong?

3 OUR LORD WALKING ON THE WATERS.— (Matt. xiv., 22-33).

B.B. Summary:—

DISPOSITIONS FOR PRAYER.

ATTENTION.   LOVE OF GOD'S WILL.
HUMILITY.   PERSEVERANCE.
            TRUST.

These and similar texts might be commented on :—

"You have not, because you ask not."— (James iv., 2).

"And all things whatsoever you shall ask in prayer, believing, you shall receive." —(Matt. xxi., 22).

" Know ye that the Lord will hear your prayers, if you continue with perseverance in fasting (acts of self-denial) and prayers in the sight of the Lord."— (Judith iv., 11).

With regard to Ejaculations, they cannot be recommended too strongly.

Each child should be encouraged to make out his own list, and to learn it by heart.

Fill several Blackboards, preferably of Indulgenced ones, for the children to choose from.

SECTION IV.

The Sacraments

Q. 255.—The Sacraments in General.

1 Hang a Crucifix before the Class.

What does Calvary mean? Our Redemption. By it we are set free—bought back.

Is there anything else needed? Yes—much.

2 As each of us came into the world, we had to be *made holy* by *Baptism.*

As we got older we had to fight for Christ, therefore we had to be *made strong,* by *Confirmation.*

In our daily life we need to be *made clean* by *Penance.*

In our daily life *we need food*—the Holy Eucharist feeds us.

Some wish to save souls for God and *become priests;* therefore they need *Holy Orders.*

Some wish *to marry* and bring up their children to serve God; therefore they need the *Sacrament of Matrimony.*

And when we come *to die,* we need help

H

on our journey, and preparation, before we see God; therefore we need *Extreme Unction*.

3 All seven Sacraments (sacred, holy things) pour grace into our souls. Where does this grace come from?

From Calvary. Our Lord allowed His Precious Blood to flow through the wounds in His Hands and Feet and Side, and thence to our souls through the seven Sacraments. (For a good diagram illustrating the above, see: " Teaching the Catechism," by the Editor of " The Sower," p. 95).

4 In all the Sacraments there is something we can see and hear; this is called the " *Outward Sign* " of the grace that the Sacrament is giving to our soul.

e.g.—When an engine driver sees a red signal he knows there is danger ahead; he can't see the danger, but the signal is an outward sign of it. So too a rash is a sign of illness; smoke of fire; tears of sorrow. Water is a sign of washing; bread of food, strength, etc. If we see water poured by a priest on a baby's head we know by this outward sign that the baby is really baptised; that whilst that water, which we can see, is being poured, God is pouring the grace, which we cannot see, into the baby's soul. If we see the Sacred Host in the priest's

hands, we know Our Lord is there, because
He said He would be—the Host is a part of
the Outward Sign.

5 The Sacraments are Our Lord's seven great
gifts to us, and He arranged all about
them before the Ascension—they are all
ordained by Him.

When you give a person a very valuable
present, you always arrange about it yourself—so did Our Lord to us.

Q. 253.—There are three Sacraments
which can only be received *once;* because
they leave a grand and noble mark on the
soul which nothing can ever take away.

The first of these great marks or seals is
given us by Baptism, and we wear it on our
souls for ever, showing Who Our Father is,
that we are the children of God.

(Once a child is solemnly adopted by anyone, no repetition of the ceremony would
have any meaning—the same is true of Baptism).

The second great mark or seal is given us
in Confirmation; by it we are stamped as belonging to God's Army—we are soldiers of
Christ—we have enlisted, and that enlisting
is made once and for all. We enter God's
army for life, and for all eternity we shall be
known by this mark as God's Soldier, who
has fought for Him.

The third great and noble mark or seal is worn by God's Priests : by it they are set aside to offer the Sacrifice.

Q. 254.—These marks are called in the Catechism "Characters." They give the character of Child of God; Soldier of God; Priest of God.

BAPTISM.

The Greek word means " washing."

Q. 256.—Its Necessity and what it does for the Soul.

Contrast the soul of a child before and after Baptism.

Before.—The child is an exile and can never get to Heaven. As it grows up the devil will have great power over it, and the child will find it very difficult to keep away from sin.

It cannot receive any of the other Sacraments.

There is no grace in its soul, so that what should be so beautiful and bright is dark and without life. This soul is the *servant* of God, but that is all.

After.—Now let us see what it is to be His *child.* All that is needed to change the mere servant into the child of God is the Sacrament of Baptism, but that is absolutely necessary. Then he who was an exile becomes an heir to the kingdom of Heaven.

The devil loses his power over that soul, and, unless that soul chooses, he will never gain it again. Grace enters, and the soul becomes so beautiful and bright that the brightest thing on earth would seem dark and ugly beside it.

When a little baby is baptised the priest says, among other things : "Receive this white garment and see thou carry it unstained before the Judgment Seat of Our Lord Jesus Christ, that thou mayest have life eternal."

Think on these words.

Baptism was perhaps instituted at the time of Our Lord's Baptism, but it only became a necessary means of salvation when Our Lord, after His Resurrection, said to His disciples : "Going therefore teach ye all nations, baptising them in the Name of the Father and of the Son and of the Holy Ghost."—(Matt. xxviii., 19).

(See too Matt. iii., 6-11). The Baptism of John was a sign of penance, but not the Sacrament.—(See Acts xix.).

If anyone died immediately after Baptism he would go straight to Heaven.

A child by Baptism becomes a member of the Church, and has a right therefore to the other Sacraments, and to all the blessings of the Church. That is why, in Baptism, we take a Saint's name—it shows we belong to the great family of the Church—just as our surname shows we belong to our earthly family.

We become too, a Christian—that is a follower of Christ. (Connect "Christening" and "chrism").

Baptism not only clothes us with the royal robe of grace, but this robe is adorned with many jewels, chiefly Faith, Hope, and Charity.

Our Baptismal Vows.

Our father and mother are called our parents, because it is to them we owe our life in this world.

We have seen that Baptism makes us the child, not of earthly parents, but of God; so when we are baptised the Church insists that someone (generally chosen by our parents), should promise, in our name, that as God is to be our Father, so we will be true children to Him. This person is called our God-parent, and it is very important that we should understand what it is he promised, as it is *we* who have to keep the promise.

He promised for us:

1 That we would never have anything to do

with the devil; never listen to what he says and, above all, never do what he suggests to us.

2 That we would have nothing to do with the devil's *works*.

His great work is the world, and by this is meant the bad part of the world, made up of those whose lives are full of lies, and who love money, self-pleasing, and amusements, more than God.

3 That we would have nothing to do with the devil's pomps.

Pomp means empty show.

The devil is very fond of pomp. You get a good example of it on the stage; it all looks so grand; a man struts about and pretends to be a king; there is a great deal of tinsel, which looks like gold, but it isn't—it is all make-believe and pretence, and so is the devil's pomp.

Therefore, when we promise in Baptism to renounce the devil and all his works and pomps, we are only promising to give up what is really of no value, and will only do us harm, but unless we pray and keep a sharp look-out, we shall make a great mistake and seize hold of the tinsel, thinking it to be gold.

CONFIRMATION.

Q. 262.—Recapitulate shortly what children already know. *Read Acts. I.*

Confirmation completes what Baptism has begun.

A baby cannot fight, but now that you are growing older, you can and you must fight for God.

A soldier needs weapons : if he had only his own two fists to fight with, he would come off badly—especially against a well-armed enemy. So too in spiritual warfare. Our Lord instituted this Sacrament of Confirmation to make us strong soldiers, well-armed against the world, against the devil, and above all, against our own selfishness.

[The time of Institution is uncertain—it was probably during the forty days of the Risen Life, and see Acts viii., 14-17. The practice of the Apostles and the teaching of the Church show that it is a Sacrament, and therefore instituted by Our Lord].

Q. 264.—Chrism is a mixture of oil of olives and balsam. It is solemnly blessed by the Bishop on Maundy Thursday.

Oil spreads, nourishes and softens : this represents the fulness of grace ; balsam preserves from corruption, and its fragrance recalls the " Good odour of Jesus Christ."

St. Cyril of Jerusalem (A.D. 347), referring to Our Lord's Baptism and to the Holy Ghost, Who descended upon Him afterwards in the likeness of a dove, says: "After you have come up from the pool of the sacred stream, to you is given the one Unction . . . wherewith Christ was anointed. But beware of supposing this to be plain Chrism; for as the bread of the Eucharist, after the invocation of the Holy Ghost, is mere bread no longer, but the body of Christ; so also this holy Chrism, after the invocation, is no more simple Chrism, nor so to say common, but the Gift of Christ, and by the presence of the Godhead, it worked in us the Holy Ghost . . . while thy body is anointed with visible Chrism, thy soul is sanctified by the Holy, Life-giving Spirit."

When you have received Confirmation, the Bishop might well say to you: "Take this holy sword, a gift from God (*i.e.*, the graces of your Confirmation), wherewith you shall overcome the adversaries of my people."— (2 Mach. 15, 16).

You are all or you hope soon to be Knights of the Blessed Sacrament. By your Confirmation you are, every one of you, Knights of God, for whom the Church prays, as She used to pray for the Knights of old on the day of their consecration.

" O Holy Lord, Almighty Father, Eternal God . . . we beseech Thy clemency that as Thou gavest strength to Thy servant Judas Maccabeus to triumph over them that invoked not Thy holy Name, so now Thou wouldst grant to this Thy servant, who has newly bowed his neck under the yoke of military service, strength and courage for the defence of faith and justice, and increase of faith, hope and charity, and wouldst give to him Thy fear and Thy love, humility, perseverance, obedience and patience."

When that prayer had been said, and the knight's sword had been girded on, he rose to his feet, brandished it three times, wiped it, as if he had already shed the blood of God's enemies, and replaced it in its scabbard.

The Bishop struck him lightly three times on the shoulder, and added:

" Be brave; be a peaceful soldier, diligent, faithful, and vowed to God."

Then the Bishop gave him a gentle blow on the cheek, with the words: " Pax tecum," and " the knight departed in peace." *

The ceremony of Confirmation should be gone through (the likeness with the above will probably attract the children's attention), and further illustration can be drawn from

---

* See " The Soldier of Christ," by Mother Mary Loyola, Burns & Oates, from which the above idea is taken.

the story of the Crusades, the Children's Crusade, etc.

Dispositions for Confirmation.

1 Knowledge of our Religion.
2 A state of grace.
3 Prayer : because we of ourselves can do nothing to prepare worthily for so great a Sacrament.

The hymns—" Come, O Creator, Spirit Blest," and " Come, Holy Ghost, Creator, come," should be learnt.

In preparation for Confirmation some " Practice " might profitably be started, of *e.g.*, obedience or self-denial, etc., etc., whereby the children might " win their spurs " and their " sword of knighthood."

The Holy Eucharist as a Sacrament.

It is well to remember that for very many of the class this will be the last time in their lives that they will study the doctrine of the Holy Eucharist.

It is therefore of vital importance to the children to get their faith and love strengthened, and their knowledge of the Church's teaching clear, definite and life-lasting.

The subject should be approached by the children with eagerness—not as something known, but as something very dear, about which they are going to learn *more*.

A very regrettable but not unknown attitude is: "The Blessed Sacrament? Oh, I know all about that." *Mere* revision is never very interesting, and it would seem better to avoid making the whole instruction consist of it.

Collect every bit of knowledge the children can give, and then tell them that that is only like a drop in the ocean compared to what there is to know about the Blessed Sacrament. Many great and holy men have spent their lives studying it, and yet have never got to the end.

Take first some part of the Doctrine with which the children are not familiar.

Names given to the Blessed Sacrament.

Holy Eucharist—means holy thanksgiving, or " giving thanks."

　　" When is the Bishop going to give thanks to-morrow?" was the way an early Christian would have asked: " What time is Mass to-morrow?"

They also spoke of it as:

　" The breaking of bread."

　The Most Holy Sacrament of the Altar.

　Viaticum. (With you on the way: provision for the journey).

Sacred Banquet.   Saving Victim.   The Hidden God.   Most dear Pelican.

Transubstantiation and Concomitance.

(Neither name need be given).

Where was Our Lord's Sacred Body at 3 o'clock on Good Friday?

Where was the Precious Blood?

Where was His Sacred Soul?

It was the Body of God, the Blood of God, the Soul of God.

But for love of us He had separated them. His blood had been shed.   His Body hung dead on the Cross.   His Soul was in Limbo.

Let us turn now to Easter Sunday:

See Him in the garden talking to Mary Magdalen; or in the Upper Room, shewing His Hands and Feet to His Apostles.   " See My Hands and My Feet.   Handle and see: for a Spirit has not flesh and bones as you see Me to have."

Obtain that now the Body, Blood, Soul and Divinity are united—*never again to be separated.*

" Christ dieth now no more : death hath no more dominion over Him."

Now we will turn to the Blessed Sacrament on the Altar.

What has the Bread been changed into? The Body of the Lord.

It is no longer bread : Our Lord said so Himself. He gave what looked like bread to His Apostles at the Last Supper, but He told them plainly : " *This* is My Body."   Of course, as He said it, it is true, and it was quite easy for Him to do it.

But since His Body is truly and really present in the Host, what else is there ? What *cannot* be separated from His Body ?   His Blood—His Soul and His Divinity.

So that when we receive Our Lord in the Sacred Host, what do we receive ?

After the words of consecration, what has the wine been changed into ?   The Blood of Our Lord.   (Refer again to Last Supper). And since His Blood is truly and really present in the Chalice, what else is there ?   His Body, Soul and Divinity.   They can never again be separated.

The custom of the Early Church of communicating the faithful under both kinds can be referred to.

Ask children to think over and bring you answers to some of the following questions :—

1 Why is the Sanctuary Lamp always kept burning before the Blessed Sacrament ?

2 Why should the Church say that it should be an oil lamp ?

3 Give some reasons for putting flowers on the Altar.

4 Find some meaning for the candles burning during Mass and Benediction.

5 When the priest brings Holy Communion to the sick, what ought to be prepared in the sick room?

6 Why do we use a Communion Cloth when going to Holy Communion?

7 Why does the Church use Incense for Benediction? What else is in the thurible?

8 How many different kinds of sacred vessels are kept in the Tabernacle?

9 Find some instances in Our Lord's Life which the Procession of Corpus Christi reminds you of, etc., etc.

EFFECTS OF HOLY COMMUNION.

Perhaps we are inclined to think that a great deal depends on us when we go to Holy Communion. In one sense this is true. We *must* be in a state of grace; we *must* want to receive Our Lord for His Sake and for our own. We *must* keep our Eucharistic fast— and then we should pray as much as we can.

The rest depends on Him. What *is* the rest?

We shall never know in this world all Our Lord does in our soul after Holy Communion, but we do know something.

He puts new life into us. Sometimes we say of a person who has come home, after being away for change of air : " She has got a new lease of life," and we mean : " She looks so much better; she is so much stronger —she can do so much more than before."

Our Lord puts His own Life into our soul— He makes us able to live that life more and more perfectly.

A little child of three can walk, but not far; a child of ten can go much further, but perhaps could not climb a mountain, whereas a strong man can.

If the life of our soul is weak we can only do easy things for God. Our Lord makes us able to do harder things for Him by giving us more and more Sanctifying Grace; this is the food of the soul, and we *must* have food if we want to be strong.

The appearances of Bread and Wine help us to understand this. Bread and wine are food, and give life and strength to the body, and Our Lord under these appearances does this for the soul.

Good food is pleasant to the taste, so does the Church sing of the Blessed Sacrament, comparing *It* to the Manna in the desert, " containing in Itself all manner of sweetness."

The Blessed Sacrament in Holy Communion remits all venial sin : all faults we commit daily, and for which we are sorry.

And moreover, according to Our Lord's promise, He sows in our souls in Holy Communion the seeds of everlasting life. This He promised when on earth : " He that eateth My Flesh and drinketh My Blood *abideth* in Me and I in him, and *I will raise him up in the last day.*" And He will keep His word.

He gives all this to our souls in Holy Communion as silently as the sun gives life and strength and beauty to the flowers by shining on them ; so we must not forget, whilst we adore and welcome Him, to thank Him too, for all He is doing at that moment in our hearts.

To learn by heart: "O Sacred Banquet, in which Christ is received, the memory of His Passion is renewed, the mind is filled with grace, and a pledge of future glory is given to us !"—(From the Liturgy).

Penance.

There will be already a fair amount of knowledge in the children's minds : this should be used to attach the fresh knowledge to.

I.—Reason for Institution.

St. John, writing about Our Lord, and thinking over some of the things He had said and done, tells us :

I

" He needed not that anyone should tell
Him for *He knew what was in Man.*"

Think over these last words for a moment,
and then tell me why you think Our Lord,
having given us Baptism, which makes our
souls as white as snow, should give us the
Sacrament of Penance as well.

A priest who had worked for years among
the Red Indians in North America, told of a
certain village, where he had instructed and
baptised the chief and the whole tribe. He
then had to leave them, and could not get
back to them till a whole year had passed.
He called them all together, found they had
been very faithful to all he had told them,
and spoke of Confession that evening, in preparation for the morning's Mass and Communion.

They were quite astonished. What could
they confess. How could they have done
again the things the Black Robe had told
them not to do? Does not the Great Spirit
hate sin? The priest added that he could
scarcely find matter for absolution among
them.

This fact might be told the children. and
they might easily answer that it is not so
always and everywhere, and that it was most
merciful and loving of Our Lord to institute
the Sacrament of Penance.

Institution.—See Matt. xvi., 19; xviii., 18; and John xx., 21-23.

This power, given by Our Lord, was to descend to the successors of the Apostles, the Bishops and Priests of the Church.—(See Matt. xxviii., 18-20).

A great gift, and one which the Church has at all times taught She possesses. It is her chief way of inviting sinners to come to her, because She does not merely comfort and help them with good advice: She actually takes their sins away and gives them back all they have lost. No other Church, of course, *can* do this: to no Church, except to His own, did Our Lord say: " Whose sins *YOU* shall forgive, they are forgiven."

PENANCE IS A SACRAMENT.

The Outward Sign is performed, partly by the person, when he goes to Confession (he accuses himself of his sins; he is sorry for them—he does his penance), and partly by the priest when he gives absolution.

It may be well to revise quickly what the children have already learnt about sin—its kinds and its effects:

What makes a sin mortal? (Use B.B.):

The thing must be in itself serious.

We must know that it is very displeasing to God.

We must deliberately choose it :

> *e.g.*, a deliberate murder.

The most important of the three things we have to do in Confession is to be sorry.

Contrition means " crushed," " broken." Great sorrow is said to crush us—to break our hearts. It is not likely that God will give us the grace of so much sorrow as that, and He does not ask it. What He does ask is that we should be seriously sorry, and for the right reason.

(Get the different reasons for sorrow from children. See p. 27, and give or get other examples).

These reasons vary very much, in some of the good ones even there is a good deal of ourselves, so there are two kinds of contrition (both good)—Perfect Contrition and Imperfect Contrition.

> " I am very sorry I have done wrong. I do want to see God in Heaven, and I certainly don't want to go to either Hell or Purgatory."

That is a very good thing to say; but still it is a question of " *I*," and where " *I* " am going to, and it is Imperfect Contrition.

> " My God, I am very sorry I have done what You hate, and what has made Our Lord suffer so much."

That is a better thing to say than the other.

We forget our own loss or gain and look at things from God's point of view—that is an act of Perfect Contrition.

It is very easy to make one. Supposing you had done something very wrong, and you were so sorry because your mother was crying about it; perhaps you could not say much, but you might kneel down beside her and try to dry her tears, and just say: "Mother." She would know how sorry you were.

Supposing you picture to yourself Calvary, and you kneel down at Our Lord's Feet; you think of what you have made Him suffer, and you just say: "Jesus," very lovingly. That is a perfect act of Contrition, and every sin is taken away—just as when you let the sun into a dark room, the darkness flees.

(Impress the point: we must love God for His own sake. Children can give examples of Perfect and Imperfect Contrition, and of sorrow which is neither).

Note the following important points on B.B.:—

1 All mortal sins *must* be confessed once, but it need only be once.

2 You are *not* bound to confess venial sins, though it is well to do so.

3 With Confession, Imperfect Contrition will
   do.
4 Perfect Contrition takes away sin *immediately* (but see No. 1).
5 At the hour of death, if a priest cannot be
   had, Perfect Contrition will do his work.

Purpose of Amendment.—The test of Contrition : " For God's sake, I wish I had not
done it, and I won't do it again."

Our Lord once described two ways of building a house : one was on a rock, the other on
sand.   He spoke too of the result in each
case (John v., 14).   Get children to apply this
to purpose of Amendment.

With regard to venial sin, in fortnightly
Confession, it is well to make a firm purpose
of amendment with regard to one class of
venial sins.   When a man wants to catch six
geese in a farmyard he runs each goose to
earth in turn, and does not try to put his arms
round the whole six at once.   So we must kill
off our habits of venial sin one by one.

Find out the *first cause* of the sin : *e.g.*—
I am very fond of talking to a certain person,
but whenever I do so, he leads me into sin.

With regard to my purpose of Amendment,
what ought my Resolution to be ?

Resolve on right means.

e.g.—" I know that unless I pray more and
go to Holy Communion oftener, I cannot

avoid that particular sin." That may be
quite true, but what Resolution will you
make if your purpose of Amendment is sincere?

Make it quite clear to the children that in
a case of mortal sins, a purpose of Amendment must be made with regard to all.

Whatever happens we must avoid *all*. If
a man has been grossly careless, with the
result that his house has been burnt down,
he does not resolve merely to avoid in future
that particular carelessness, but *all fire*, from
whatever cause.

Circumstances which lead to sin are called
occasions of sin, and these we must avoid as
far as we can.

We had one example in the boy who led
his friend into sin. Can you give others?

(Bad books, certain places of amusement,
a master who prevents attendance at Sunday
Mass, etc.).

What is the answer to this Proverb?

"Can a man walk on hot coals and his
feet not be burnt?"—(Proverbs vi.,
28).

What does it mean?

Some of these circumstances we may be
able to avoid, some not: *e.g.*—the Judges and
Prefects who threatened the early Christians
with horrible tortures and death if they did

136THEFAITHFORCHILDREN

not commit idolatry were "occasions of sin" to the martyrs, which they could not avoid, and against these they had to arm themselves by prayer and Holy Communion: thus the "occasion of sin" became the occasion of their salvation.

QUALITIES OF CONFESSION. *(On B.B.)*.

1 HUMBLE: I must blame myself really; I am a sinner.

2 SHORT: The kind of Sin. Number of times if sin is serious, and circumstances which change the kind of sin:

> *e.g.*—I have told lies—three times— once it injured someone's character."

3 SINCERE AND ENTIRE: The truth, the whole truth, and nothing but the truth.

"And David said to Nathan: I have sinned against the Lord; and Nathan said: The Lord also has taken away thy sin; thou shalt not die."—(2 Kings, xii., 13).

The answer comes quickly after the accusation.

The account of Ananias and Saphira (Acts v., 1-11) is worth studying with the children. Also some verses of Psalm 50.

To accuse oneself means to bring a charge against oneself.

To absolve means to let loose.

To retain sin means to refuse Absolution.

EXAMINATION OF CONSCIENCE.

The children will have been taught to examine their conscience every evening at Night Prayers; the total result is all that is wanted for the fortnightly Confession.

They should be trained to be business-like about this Examination, and to realise that it is really a very simple thing, to be done simply and seriously.

Their weekly Order of Day, with special reference to Saturday and Sunday, is generally speaking sufficient to ' serve as a framework and reminder.

They might, perhaps, be warned against the wearisome wading through of Questions on the 16 Commandments, still found in some prayer books, and of no utility in their case.

EFFECTS OF ABSOLUTION. *(On B.B.).*

1 It forgives all sin.

2 It gives back Sanctifying Grace, if lost through mortal sin.

3 It increases Sanctifying Grace, if it is already in the soul.

4 It does away with eternal punishment, if this has been deserved.

5 It does away with some, if not all, temporal punishment.

6 It joins the soul again to the Communion of

Saints, if that soul, through mortal sin, had been cut off.

7 It gives actual graces, to avoid sin in the future.

SATISFACTION. *(On B.B.)*.

Every sin is punished sooner or later—
  Either in this world,
      or in Purgatory—TEMPORAL PUNISH-MENT.
  or (if not repented of) in Hell—ETERNAL PUNISHMENT.
Punishment or Satisfaction in this World.
  It may be :

1 The penance given us by the Priest in Confession.
    This is part of the Sacrament, and it has the Precious Blood joined with it.

2 Holy Mass, Prayers and the Indulgences which we gain.

3 The sufferings or crosses, which God sends or allows, and which we bear patiently.

4 Other good deeds which we perform.

When sin is forgiven the guilt is gone, never to return, but the punishment remains—a debt which we have to pay. If the Church grants us Indulgences, She Herself is paying off some of our debt.

If we gain a Plenary Indulgence the whole

debt is paid off; if we gain a Partial Indulgence a part of the debt is paid off.

Canonical Penances.—In the early days of the Church the penance given for big sins was very long and very hard.

The penitents, as they were called, knelt outside the Church dressed in black, and were not allowed to enter, nor to receive Holy Communion.

Some who had fallen away in the last Persecution and had repented, knelt there all their lives, unless they were granted an Indulgence—a Plenary one, *i.e.*, they were let off a life-time penance. Some had to kneel there and do penance for other sins: some for a year, some for forty days (Quarantine), or seven years, and so on.

The Penance the Church now gives is very small, but the Priest gives us Absolution on condition we do it: say your Penance before leaving the Church after Confession.

Indulgences applicable to Souls in Purgatory.

The Church, by Indulgences, not only pays off our debts, but She wants us to pay off some of the debts of the souls in Purgatory.

The souls in Purgatory can no longer gain Indulgences, so it is a great act of charity to gain some for them.

Supposing a friend of yours had got into debt. He owed, let us say, £1. His father forgave him, but told him he would have to earn the money, and then pay him back. He can only earn 2s. a week—that means ten weeks' work.

You happen to know all about it, and give him 4s., thus he is let off two weeks' work.

Supposing a soul is to be in Purgatory for ten weeks more—you gain a Partial Indulgence for that soul. God perhaps lets it off two weeks out of the ten (you cannot tell how much). That is like paying the 4s. out of the £1 for your friend.

THANKSGIVING AFTER CONFESSION.

Get suggestions from the children.

The Divine Praises make a good Thanksgiving.

Also Psalm 102 :

" Bless the Lord O my soul, and let all that is within me praise His holy Name.

Bless the Lord O my soul, and never forget all that He has done for thee."

Recommend your purpose of Amendment to Our Lady and to your Angel Guardian and Patron Saint. Ask them to remind you of it.

EXTREME UNCTION.

On Easter Sunday evening, if you remember, when the sun was almost setting, two of Our Lord's disciples were standing at the door of an inn with Him. He was making a sign as if He meant to go on further, but they pressed Him to remain, saying : " Stay with us, for it is towards evening, and the day is now far spent."

We may look on our life as a day, and when evening comes we have to die.

For some, life is a long day, for others short—we cannot even guess how long it will be—but whatever the length, evening is sure to come, for we must all die. When it comes we too shall say to Our Lord : " Stay with me, for it is towards evening, and I dare not die alone."

Our Lord is very anxious about our death, because if that is right, all will be right for ever, and Our Lord cares a great deal about what is so important for us.

And, as you know, He has given us a Sacrament to help us whenever we are dangerously ill, and above all at the great moment of our last illness and death.

Effects of Extreme Unction.

1 It comforts and strengthens our soul, preparing it for its last journey.

2 It forgives venial sin and increases Sanctifying Grace.

3 It destroys the *remains of sin* already forgiven. That is:

> The temporal punishment due to sin.
>
> The inclination of our heart to sin.
>
> Spiritual weakness of soul, which makes it difficult for it to raise itself to God.
>
> (These are either entirely destroyed or lessened according as to whether our love for God is very great or less great).

4 It soothes our ˙bodily pain and sometimes brings us back to health—but this depends on whether God sees it to be good for us or not.

Get children to realise that Extreme Unction should be given *as early as possible* in any dangerous illness:—*(a)* because it is then easier for a sick person to receive it with devotion; *(b)* it will more easily restore health; *(c) no one* can tell the moment of death. We should *never* delay its reception.

(On B.B.)—

Extreme Unction forgives Mortal Sin indirectly:

Imperfect Contrition joined to Extreme Unction will forgive mortal sin, when Confession is impossible—*e.g.*, when a person is unconscious.

Make it clear to the children that as many

people have imperfect (not perfect) Contrition in their hearts, if they are struck down suddenly and are in danger of death, the most urgent thing to do is to get the Priest.

It is clear from the above that if such persons were in mortal sin, but with Imperfect Contrition in their hearts when they were struck down, Extreme Unction will save them.

This very important doctrine, well learnt, may help the children during life to save more than one soul.

> Extreme Unction is a Sacrament of the living, and must be received in a state of grace—it does not (except indirectly) forgive mortal sin.

Penance is the Sacrament that does this. Extreme Unction means " the last anointing." The Church has anointed us in Baptism and in Confirmation : now She is going to anoint us for the last time, and make us holy for eternity.

The oil used is oil of olives, blessed for the purpose by the Bishop on Maundy Thursday.

The Priest comes to our room bearing the Holy Oils and the Blessed Sacrament. As he enters, he says : " Peace be to this house," to which the server answers : "And to all who dwell therein."

The Priest places the Blessed Sacrament and the Holy Oils on our little altar, gives us

a Crucifix to kiss, sprinkles the room and all
who are in it with Holy Water, and then we
make our Confession to him; after which the
Confiteor is said, and then the Priest gives
us our last Communion, which, as you know,
the Church calls " Viaticum " (provision for
the Way: with you on the Way). The words
he says are changed :" Receive my brother
(or sister) the Viaticum of the Body of Our
Lord Jesus, to guard you from the malignant
Enemy, and lead you to life eternal."

The Priest then changes his white stole for
purple, and gives us the Sacrament of Extreme Unction.

He anoints our eyes, ears, nostrils, lips,
hands and feet; and as he does so he says
each time : " By this holy anointing and by
His most tender mercy, may the Lord forgive
thee all the sins thou hast committed by thy
sight (hearing, etc.). If the person's last
moment seems very close at hand, the Priest
anoints the forehead only, and then if there is
time the senses.

At the end he will give us the "Apostolic
Blessing " for the hour of death. This is the
Blessing of Our Holy Father the Pope, to
which a Plenary Indulgence is attached.

All we have to do is to lie still; offer our
life willingly to God, love Him and trust Him.
He has come into our souls so often in life,

and now he has come to take us on our last
journey into eternity. We are safe with Him,
and He will be our light if it is dark, and our
comfort if the pain is sharp. He is well able
to take care of us.

We commend our death to Our Lady every
time we say the Hail Mary. She will be at
our side then, so too our Angel Guardian.

Sometimes when we are tempted to sin,
let us think of this last scene, and ask ourselves : " What shall I wish *then* that I had
done *now?*"

HOLY ORDERS.

When a boy wants to become a Priest, what
does it mean ? That he wants to receive the
Sacrament of Holy Orders; to receive the
power Our Lord gave His Apostles.

These powers are :

1 To say Mass: given at the Last Supper :
   "Do this in commemoration of Me."—
   (Luke xxii., 19).

   God bade the Apostles do it, therefore
   He gave them the power.

2 To forgive sins: given on Easter Sunday
   evening: "Receive ye the Holy Ghost;
   whose sins you shall forgive they are forgiven, whose sins you shall retain, they
   are retained."—(John xx., 21-23).

3 To teach and to baptise: given before the
   Ascension: "All power is given to Me
   K

in Heaven and on earth : Go ye therefore, teach ye all nations, baptising them
in the Name of the Father and of the Son
and of the Holy Ghost, teaching them to
observe whatsoever I have commanded
you, and behold I am with you all days,
even to the consummation of the world."
—(Matt. xxviii., 18-20).

4 To do all other priestly work entrusted to
him by the Bishop. (The children can
suggest).

A great deal of preparation, of hard study
and of prayer is, of course, necessary, but if
the boy continued to persevere in his desire,
then the day would come, when he would be
given by the Bishop what are known as Minor
Orders.

There would be first of all the ceremony of
the Tonsure; not an Order, but a preparatory
rite, showing that he who wishes to be a
Priest is separated from the world.

Then he would receive Minor Orders, four
in number :

PORTER : a dangerous office in the early
Church, when the pagans would often
break through the door and carry off the
Christians.

LECTOR : he has the right to read parts of
the Scriptures to the Faithful at certain
ceremonies.

Exorcist : he had the power of chasing away the devil—but only Priests and Bishops may now exercise this power. The sensible presence of the devil is less common than it was before the Incarnation. The children can give instances of this kind of miracle worked by Our Lord.

Acolyte.—The children can give an account of his duties.

After the Cleric, who wanted to be a Priest, had received these four Minor Orders, some time would elapse, longer or shorter, according to the wish of the Bishop, which he would spend in prayer and study before he received the first Major Order—the Subdiaconate.— See Acts vi., 1-8.

Tell how in the early Church the Faithful received Holy Communion after a supper, which they took together, in imitation of Our Lord and His disciples at the Last Supper. When the repast was over the Deacons, who had presided at it, distributed Holy Communion.

A year elapses between the reception of the Subdiaconate and the Diaconate. The Subdeacon's chief duty is to serve the Deacon at High Mass, just as the Deacon's chief duty is to serve the Bishop or Priest at High Mass.

Another year would pass by, and the

greatest day of a Priest's life would come at last, and he would be ordained Priest.

Get children to explain the text: " Thou art a Priest for ever according to the Order of Melchisedech."

Make it clear that there is only *one* Sacrament of Holy Orders, but it is conferred in three degrees, giving more and more power: Deacon—Priest—Bishop.

The Sub-diaconate and Minor Orders were instituted by the Church.

Revise what was said about the " Character " of the Priesthood conferred by the Sacrament.

Speak in season of the dignity and beauty of the Priesthood and of the gift of vocation.

" Neither doth any man take the honour to himself, but he that is called by God, as Aaron was."—(Heb. v., 4).

" You have not chosen *Me*, but *I* have chosen you."—(John xv., 16).

ORDERS AND JURISDICTION.

These we must distinguish:

By Orders, as we have seen, a Priest receives the power to offer Sacrifice and administer five of the Sacraments;

A Bishop at his Consecration receives the *power* to admíster all seven;

But neither have the *right* to do so, unless they receive Jurisdiction:

    Orders give the power;

    Jurisdiction gives the right.

The Church received both from Our Lord; Universal Jurisdiction was given to the Apostles by the words: " Go ye, and teach *all* nations."

Only the Pope has Universal Jurisdiction. He receives it direct from Our Lord.

The Bishops receive Jurisdiction from the Pope over a part of a country, called a Diocese.

A Priest receives Jurisdiction from the Bishop to whose Diocese he belongs, over a town or part of a town situated within that Diocese.

Note that a Priest can only hear Confessions in that place named by the Bishop, except in the case of the dying.

Every Priest *everywhere* can absolve *anyone* who is in danger of death.

There is a beautiful description of an Ordination and First Mass in " The King's Achievement," by Mgr. Hugh Benson (Part II. of Book II., chap. 2).

MATRIMONY.

Recall the miracle of Cana.—(John ii., 1-11).

Marriage is a contract and a *Sacrament.*

(a) *A Contract, i.e.,* an agreement made with full consent, not merely between man and woman, but between God and the man and woman.

No contract is of any binding force unless made under authority, and in the way that that authority lays down, *e.g.,* receipts for large sums of money are valueless unless stamped, etc.   Now, as Matrimony is a God-man Contract, and a Sacrament, the only lawful Authority is the Church.

She has decreed (Easter 1908) that Catholics must be married before the Parish Priest, or a Priest approved of by him; and there must be two witnesses. (Explain that this is true, even if only one of the parties is Catholic).

Since these are the Church's conditions, and that the Contract is made under Her Authority, it is clear that no marriage made any other way is a *marriage at all.*

The great point to remember is that it is a question for the Church to settle, and that what Catholics have to do is to tell the Priest *in good time*—three months beforehand if possible—and do what he says.

(b) *A Sacrament:* Our Blessed Lord raised the contract to the dignity of a Sacrament perhaps at Cana, perhaps later.—(See Matt. xix., 4-6).

St. Paul, speaking of Matrimony, says: "This is a great Sacrament."—(Eph. v., 32).

Since Our Lord's time, it is not possible for a Christian to make the Contract, without also receiving the Sacrament.

Inward Grace.—It is a Sacrament of the living, and must therefore be received in a state of Grace; it increases Sanctifying Grace and gives Grace that those who receive it should serve God holily in the married state, love one another and make their children good Catholics. These graces will be at hand all their lives—ready just when they want them—like a big sum of money they can draw from when they want.

Matrimony is a very holy state, sanctified by one of God's greatest gifts (a Sacrament).

The Church wishes Her children to receive Holy Communion on their wedding day. She also wishes the Nuptial Mass to be said, and the Church's special Blessing to be given to the Bride and Bridegroom after the Pater Noster, and again after the " Ite Missa Est."

Mixed Marriages. Sometimes Catholics want to marry non-Catholics. This the Church forbids and dislikes very much, though sometimes She gives leave, for grave reasons. She never allows a Mixed Marriage

unless the non-*Catholic* *promises* *perfect*
freedom to the Catholic in the practice of
Religion, and that all the children shall be
brought up Catholics.

It is not a promising beginning for people
who are going to live together all their life in
love and harmony, to begin by disagreeing
on the most important points.

*Marriage lasts till the death of husband or
    wife.*

Divorce, of which you have heard, is
allowed by the laws of this and other coun-
tries, but remember Matrimony is a Sacrament, and so the Civil Law can neither make
nor unmake it.   (Dissolve means to untie).

There is no such thing as divorce for Catholics; Our Lord forbade it, when He came—
for Moses had allowed it to the Jews (because
of their hardness of heart, Our Lord said),
and He added : " What God hath joined together let no man put asunder."—(Matt. xix.,
3-6; 1 Cor., vii., 10, 11).

When the Priest blesses the wedding ring,
he prays that the two people may love one
another always.

A word might be said of what the Church
has suffered in defence of this Sacrament,
e.g., under Henry VIII., because She upheld
his marriage with Katherine of Arragon, or
at the hands of Napoleon, because She upheld

the marriage of his brother Jerome, to Miss Paterson.

SACRAMENTALS.—*(Use B.B.).*

Sacraments :

An outward sign of inward grace.

Instituted by Jesus Christ.

They *infallibly* give grace unless the recipient puts an obstacle in the way.

Sacramentals :

An outward sign of inward grace.

Instituted by the Church.

The grace they give depends on the blessing of the Church, and the dispositions of those who make use of them.

Examples of Sacramentals :

The use of Holy Water; Ashes on Ash Wednesday.

Striking the breast at the Confiteor, at Mass.

Almsgiving when prescribed by the Church, *e.g.*, during Lent.

Blessings given by the Pope, Bishops, Priests, etc., etc.

Effects of Sacramentals :

i. The remission of venial sin, if accompanied with contrition.

ii. Remission of temporal punishment.

iii. The subduing or putting to flight the devil.

iv. Temporal blessings.

SECTION V.

THE HOLY SACRIFICE OF THE MASS

NATURE OF SACRIFICE : SACRIFICES UNDER THE OLD LAW.

Get the children to find, from the answer in the Catechism, what constitutes a Sacrifice.

VICTIM—PRIEST—OFFERING TO GOD ALONE.

Reason.—Because He is the Sovereign Lord of all things.

> *Sacrifices before Moses.*—*e.g.*, Cain and Abel : " Cain offered of the fruits of the earth ; gifts to the Lord : Abel also offered of the firstlings of his flock.— (Gen. iv., 3, 4).
>
> *Noe :* after the deluge.—(Gen. viii., 20, 21).
>
> *Abraham* offered the sacrifice of a cow, a goat, a ram, a turtle and a pigeon, at the command of God Himself.
>
> *Melchisedech*, the High Priest of God, offered a sacrifice of bread and wine.

So that evidently from the beginning, God gave man the idea of giving Him things ; offering things to Him, which He accepted.

When Moses received the Commandments from God, he was taught the different kinds of Sacrifice which were to be made to God.

There were bloody and unbloody Sacrifices.

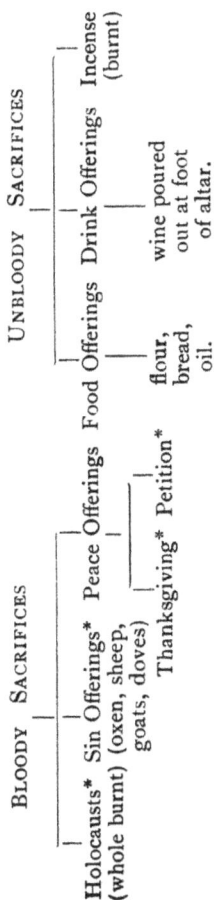

BLOODY SACRIFICES
- Holocausts* (whole burnt) (oxen, sheep, goats, doves)
- Sin Offerings*
- Peace Offerings
  - Thanksgiving*
  - Petition*

UNBLOODY SACRIFICES
- Food Offerings — flour, bread, oil.
- Drink Offerings — wine poured out at foot of altar.
- Incense (burnt)

* Note in above the four great ends of Sacrifice.

Morning and Evening Sacrifice.—The trumpets were blown; Psalms were sung; a lamb was sacrificed; food offerings were made, and wine was poured out.

All these Sacrifices were types of the One Great Sacrifice of the New Law. They ceased when Our Lord came, and the Holy Mass took their place. They were only pleasing to God as types, not as realities.

Refer to the Sacrifice of Isaac by Abraham (Gen. xxii., 1-18), and to the Sacrifice of the Paschal Lamb (Exodus xii., 1-11), as two other very perfect types.

Malachias, the last of the Prophets, in order of time, whose name means: "the Angel of the Lord," lived about 400 years before Our Lord. He foretold Our Lord's coming, and made the most famous of all the prophecies concerning the Holy Mass.

"For from the rising of the sun, even to the going down of the same, My Name is great among the Gentiles, and in every place there is Sacrifice, and there is offered to My Name a clean Oblation, saith the Lord of Hosts."

There is no moment of the day in which the Holy Sacrifice is not being offered.

THE HOLY MASS AND CALVARY.

Calvary is the same Sacrifice as the Holy Mass.

	CALVARY	HOLY MASS (on B.B.)
THE PRIEST.	Jesus Christ, Who offers Himself to His Eternal Father.	Jesus Christ, Who offers Himself, through the hands of His Priests.
THE VICTIM.	Jesus Christ. His mortal Body.	Jesus Christ. His immortal glorified Body.
TO WHOM?	To the Eternal Father.	To the Eternal Father,
HOW?	By the actual shedding of His Blood.	In an unbloody manner.
WHY?	To give God supreme honour. To give God supreme thanks. To obtain pardon for sin. To obtain all we need.	To give God supreme honour. To give God supreme thanks, To obtain pardon for sin. To obtain all we need.
WHEN?	Once on Good Friday.	Daily and thousands of times a day.
WHERE?	On Mount Calvary.	Throughout the world.
RESULT?	Redemption of the world.	Application of that Redemption to individual souls.

The children will notice that there is one great difference between the two Sacrifices of

Calvary and the Mass, and that is the difference between a bloody and an unbloody Sacrifice.

The Essence of the Sacrifice.

In what does the essence of the Mass consist ?

(This requires slow and careful teaching
and a good deal of repetition before the children have made the doctrine their own).

What do we mean by the essence of a thing ?
That by which a thing is—without which it
would not be. Flour and water are the
essence of bread—separated there is no
bread : salt may be added, but it is not of the
essence of it.

The union of soul and body are the essence
of man : to have, *e.g.*, two arms, is necessary
to make him perfect, but the loss of one or
two arms would not prevent his being a man.

What now is the essence of the Mass, without which it would not be Mass ?

The twofold Consecration—*(a)* of the
bread ; *(b)* of the wine :

In the former, after the Consecration, *Our
Lord's Body* is present, and because It can-
not be separated from His Body : His Soul,
Blood and Divinity :

In the latter, after the second Consecration,
His Precious Blood is present, and because

they cannot be separated from the Blood :
His Body, Soul and Divinity.

On Calvary the Blood was really separated
from His Body, because He shed it *all :* the
last drops escaped from His Heart when the
soldier pierced His Side and His death was
brought about by the shedding of His Blood.

In the Mass there is separation, *though only
in appearance*, by the two-fold Consecration.

By the power of the words of Consecration,
the *Body* of the Lord is present in the Host.
His Soul and Blood are only present, because
they cannot be separated from His Body.

By the power of the words of Consecration,
the Blood is present in the Chalice : His Body
and Soul are only present because they cannot be separated from His Blood—therefore
there is an *appearance* of separation.

It is, of course, always the Body of *God*,
the Blood of *God*, the Soul of *God*, and we
must remember too that it is His *Glorified
Body* that is present.

So that on the Altar we have a representation of what took place on Calvary :

On Calvary the separation was real—that
is to say, Calvary was a Bloody Sacrifice : in
the Holy Mass it is apparent : set forth before
our eyes, to be done " in commemoration of
Him."

This is what the Church means when She

says Our Lord offers Himself to the Eternal Father on the Altar, in an *unbloody manner:*

The appearances of bread and wine are not offered, but the God-made-Man.

It is Jesus Christ Who is the Victim, and He offers Himself to God alone.

Make it clear that Mass may be said in honour of Our Lady and of the Saints, and prayers may be said to them during it, but the Mass cannot be offered to them because it is the Sacrifice of the New Law, and " a Sacrifice is offered to God alone, in testimony of His being the sovereign Lord of all things."

In the Mass, we offer to the Eternal Father :

A Holocaust. A Sacrifice of adoration, praise, and perfect homage.

A Sacrifice of Thanksgiving. Eucharistic : it fully pays our debt of thanks.

A Sacrifice for Sin. The Mass does not forgive sin directly, but it obtains for us the grace of contrition and repentance.

A Sacrifice of Petition to obtain through Jesus Christ from His Eternal Father, all we need for soul and body.

(All foreshadowed under the Old Law.—See p. 155).

Our Lord in the Mass is the true Priest. Who offers Himself as Victim.

The Priest who says Mass is His Minister, who lends Him, as it were, his voice and his hands, without which Mass would not now be possible.

We all join with the Priest in offering the Sacrifice, offered in the name of the whole Church militant.

Before the Preface, the Priest turns to the people and says: "Pray, brethren, that my Sacrifice *and yours* may be acceptable to God the Father Almighty."

The Holy Mass may be offered for (i.e., its fruits may be applied to) :—

 i. The person who caused the Mass to be offered, or the person for whom the Priest offers It.

 ii. For all the Living, not merely the Faithful.

 iii. For the Souls in Purgatory.

 iv. To honour Our Lady and the Saints or some particular Saint, and thus obtain their intercession for us.

Explain meaning of the offering made to the Priest, who at the request of the Faithful, says Mass for their intention :

" They who preach the Gospel shall live by the Gospel."—(1 Cor., ix., 14).

L

Vestments.

Every one of the Vestments worn by the Priest has a meaning, generally referring to Our Lord's Passion, if not, to some virtue He practised :

Amice.—A square piece of linen, placed by the Priest first on his head and then round his neck. It reminds us of the cloth with which the soldiers blindfolded Our Lord.

Alb.—A white linen robe, representing the fool's white garment with which Herod clothed Our Lord—the Eternal Wisdom.

Girdle.—The Priest fastens it round his waist and gathers in the Alb. It reminds us of the cords with which Our Lord was bound, and the scourges used.

Maniple.—Worn by the Priest on his left arm. It represents the rope with which Our Lord's Hands were tied.

Stole.—A long narrow piece of silk, worn over the shoulders and crossed on the breast. A sign of spiritual authority, representing the yoke of Christ; therefore the Priest kisses it before putting it on, to show that Our Lord's yoke is, as He Himself said, sweet.

Chasuble.—The outer Vestment, made of silk, almost covering the body : representing the Cross of Christ and Charity.

Colours of Vestments.

White: on the joyful mysteries of Our Lord's Life; on the Feasts of Our Lady, and of Confessors and Virgins.   It represents joy and purity.

Red: on the Feasts of the Passion, on Whit Sunday (emblem of fire), and on the Feasts of all Martyrs.

Green: the colour of Hope, used at times which have no particular colour of their own—*e.g.*, between the Epiphany and Septuagesima, and after Pentecost till Advent.

Purple: an emblem of Penance, worn during Lent and Advent and on Vigils.

Black: the sign of mourning; worn on Good Friday and in Masses for the Dead.

Note.—The following notes on the Ordinary of the Mass have been made out in full for the convenience of the teacher, but it is suggested that the children should be got to find out all they possibly can for themselves.   This might be the work of many weeks, the result of attention during Sunday Mass, etc., but it would be far more valuable and better remembered, than if given by the teacher at instruction.

Every child should, however, be quite familiar with everything in these notes before the year's work is finished.

MASS IS SAID IN LATIN—and Latin is the language for all the ceremonies of the Western Church. Why?

Unity is, as you know, a mark of the Church, and to preserve that unity, Mass may only be said in the language prescribed by the Church. This, for the Western half of the world, is Latin; for the Eastern half, Greek, Syriac, Coptic, or Slavonic is used.

The Church *might*, of course, if She thought it wise, order that Mass should be said in the language of the country, but it is not likely that She will, for the reason given above.

Ordinary of the Mass

The children should become perfectly familiar with the principal parts of the Mass, and be able to follow it easily.

By degrees they should learn to link the different parts of the Mass to the different stages in Our Lord's Passion :

> (a) The Altar raised on high in the Church, and several steps leading up to it. (Latin—" altus," high or raised).
>
> (Calvary and the ascent to it).
>
> (b) The Priest enters, wearing vestments marked with a Cross.
>
> (He represents Christ, Who bore His Cross for us).

I.—Preparation for the Sacrifice.

At the foot of the Altar.—The Psalm " Judge
me, O God " (Psalm 42), composed by
King David after his sin and its punishment : *i.e.*, the rebellion of his son Absa-
lom. A Psalm of contrition and sorrow.
Acts of humility and contrition.

The Confiteor and some Invocations.

The Priest ascends the Altar and kisses it,
in honour of the relics of the martyrs con-
tained within the Altar-stone.

II.—Entrance to the Mass.

Introit.—A passage from Holy Scripture, a
verse of a Psalm and the Gloria Patri
(read one or two to the children). The
Introit gives the characteristic note of
the Mass which is to follow, *e.g.*—joy,
sorrow, penance, etc.

Kyrie.—Three triple invocations for mercy :
thrice in honour of the Father, thrice in
honour of the Son, thrice in honour of
the Holy Spirit.

Gloria—Obtain the origin of the opening
words.—The Church's greatest hymn of
praise (author unknown). The Gloria is
omitted in penitential seasons and in
Masses for the Dead.

The children might suggest an explanation

of each sentence of the Gloria in Excelsis, either orally or in writing.

III.—FROM THE GLORIA TO THE GOSPEL.

1 *Dominus Vobiscum.*—The Priest's salutation to the people and their response (Ruth. ii., 4). It occurs at intervals during the Mass (five times in all).

2 *The Collect.*—Said like the Introit at the Epistle side of the Altar. It is a prayer, beginning with: " Let us pray," which invites us all to join with the Priest. The Collect *collects* in the mouth of the Priest the needs and wishes of the Congregation.

3 *The Epistle.*—A passage taken from any portion of the Holy Scriptures, except the Psalms and the four Gospels, but it is generally taken from the Epistles (Letters) of the Apostles, written during their lifetime to the different Christian Churches.

4 *The Gradual*—(gradus means a step).—So called because it used to be sung from the first step of the Altar. Generally it consists of two verses of one of the Psalms.

IV.—THE GOSPEL AND THE CREED.

1 Before the Gospel· the Priest says a preparatory prayer, bowing profoundly before the Altar.

Gospel means " good tidings of God." At High Mass the Church shows Her veneration for the Gospel by incense and lights. Only a Priest or Deacon is allowed to sing it at Mass.

2 *The Creed*, which follows the Gospel, is a solemn act of Faith in the whole of God's revelation to man. It is said on Sundays, on all Feasts of Our Lord and of His Mother, and on all the great Feasts of Saints.

Except Our Lady, St. Mary Magdalen is the only woman Saint on whose Feast a Creed is said throughout the Church.

Many phrases and special words in the Creed furnish very interesting and profitable exercises for the children (oral or written)—*e.g.*, Maker, only begotten Son, Light of Light, Lord and Life-Giver, etc.

V.—From the Offertory to the Preface.

1 *The Offertory* is an Antiphon. It was here that the Faithful, in olden times, used to make offerings of bread and wine.

2 *The things offered by the Priest* are bread and wine. The Priest mingles a drop or two of water with the wine, because Our Lord did so at the Last Supper, and the mixture of wine and water represents the

blood and water which flowed from His Side when the soldier pierced it.

The Priest first offers the Host lying on the paten, then he offers the wine in the Chalice, joins his hands upon the Altar and says two more prayers, begging of God to accept the offerings.

3 *The Washing of the Hands.*—The Priest here recites the 25th Psalm. This is a sign of the perfect purity required for the Holy Sacrifice. Only the thumb and the forefinger are washed—*i.e.*, the part of the hand consecrated on the Priest's ordination day.

(Pilate's act of hypocrisy is *not* here commemorated).

4 The Priest returns to the middle of the Altar, joins his hands, and bows slightly, praying for the fifth time that God would accept his offering.

5 *Orate Fratres.*—After kissing the Altar the Priest prays, turns to the Faithful, and asks them to pray with him that his and their Sacrifice may be pleasing to God.

6 *Secret.*—So-called because said in a low voice. A prayer asking for the graces we require.

(Read one or two to the children).

VI.—THE PREFACE TO THE CONSECRATION.

1 *The Preface* is the introduction to the
Canon. It is to thank God for all His
mercies and to unite ourselves to the
Angels in their songs before the Throne
of God.

(The children would do well to learn the
Common Preface by heart).

N.B.—It is only the middle part of the
Preface which changes. There are eleven
Prefaces in all.

2 *The Canon* of the Mass means the fixed part
of the Mass, *i.e.*, that part which does not
change. (The Canon of Scripture is the
fixed List of Books which the Church
recognises as inspired. The word Canon
in its origin meant a fixed rod).

It consists first of Our Lord's own words;
secondly of prayers received from the
traditions of the Apostles; thirdly of
prayers ordered by different Popes.
There has been no addition to the Canon
since the time of St. Gregory the Great
(1400 years ago).

(Early in the 19th century a petition was
sent to Rome, asking that St. Joseph's
name might be added to those of Our
Lady and the Martyrs in the Canon, but
the request was refused).

The first Prayer of the Canon contains the commemoration of the living :—(i.) for the Holy Catholic Church : (ii.) for the Holy Father ; (iii.) ; for the Bishop ; (iv.) —by name—for those whom the Priest wishes to pray for, and (v.), " for all here present."

This prayer ends with the commemoration of Our Lady and of the Saints in Glory.

3 *The Priest spreads* his hands over the oblation of bread and wine, and the thumbs are stretched one over the other in the form of a cross. In the Old Law this gesture signified the transfer of something to another—in this case it shows the transfer of the sins of the world to Our Lord, Who died for them on the Cross.

4 *The Priest blesses the bread and wine five times*, and begs that this oblation may become for us the Body and Blood of Our Lord Jesus Christ.

VII.—The Consecration.

1 *Of the Bread.*—The Priest recalls " the day before He suffered," when He took bread, and gave to His disciples, saying : This is My Body.

2 *Of the Wine.*—" In like manner after He had supped, taking also this excellent

Chalice . . . He gave to His disciples,
saying: Take and drink ye all of this:
FOR THIS IS THE CHALICE OF MY BLOOD
OF THE NEW AND ETERNAL TESTAMENT,
THE MYSTERY OF FAITH, WHICH SHALL BE
SHED FOR YOU AND FOR MANY TO THE
REMISSION OF SINS."

Both the Host and the Chalice are elevated,
each in turn, and a bell is rung to warn
us to make our act of Faith and Adoration, with our eyes fixed on the Sacred
Host, and the words on our lips of St.
Thomas—" My Lord and My God."

To this an Indulgence is attached: our
act of Faith is greater than St. Thomas's,
for we do not see Our Lord's Sacred
Humanity as He did. The Holy Eucharist remains: " *the Mystery of Faith.*"

VIII.—FROM THE CONSECRATION TO THE
PATER NOSTER.

1 The prayers said in silence by the Priest
offer to the Eternal Father, " a pure
Victim, a holy Victim, an immaculate
Victim, the holy Bread of eternal life,"
and beg that all present may through
Jesus Christ " be filled with all heavenly
blessing and grace."

We can hardly do better than join in this
prayer.

2 The Priest prays for all the faithful departed, and mentions those he particularly wishes to pray for.

3 The Priest raises his voice slightly and you can hear the Latin words, which mean: "And to us sinners" . . . He prays that a share may be granted to us in the lot of the Saints; "through Him and with Him and in Him is to Thee, God the Father, in the Unity of the Holy Ghost, all honour and Glory."

4 The last words of this prayer are said aloud by the Priest: "for ever and ever," to which the people answer: AMEN, through the server or choir.

IX.—FROM THE PATER NOSTER TO THE COMMUNION.

1 *The Our Father*, preceded by the words: "Instructed by Thy divine precepts and following Thy divine institution, we dare to say Our Father," etc.

St. Jerome tells us that Our Lord Himself told His Apostles that the Pater was to be said immediately after the Consecration.

It is well to say the "Our Father" at all times, but best of all with the Priest, in the Holy Sacrifice.

2 *The Breaking of the Host.*—The Priest

breaks the Sacred Host into two, then he breaks off a small portion of one half and drops it into the Chalice, so that it is mingled with the Blood.

The practice of breaking the Host comes from the institution of Christ and the example of the Apostles.

In the early Church the celebration of Mass and Holy Communion were spoken of always as " the breaking of Bread," and the Evangelists record how Our Lord " took bread, blessed and *brake it*."

Remind the children that Our Lord's Body is glorified in the Blessed Sacrament, and cannot therefore be touched by what is done to the Host.

" May this mingling and consecration of the Body and Blood of Our Lord Jesus Christ be to us who receive It, effectual to eternal life."

3 *The Agnus Dei.*—The Priest covers the Chalice, genuflects, and rises; then says three times the "Agnus Dei" (John i., 29) : He is the true Lamb, who has taken away the sins of the world.

4 *Three prayers before Holy Communion.*— The first is for peace; the second and third are the Priest's immediate preparation for Holy Communion.

X.—From the Priest's Communion to the
end of Mass.

1 *The Priest's Communion.*—Before communicating the Priest says : " I will take
the Bread of Heaven and call upon the
Name of the Lord," then taking the
Host and Paten in his left hand, he
strikes his breast with his right hand, and
says three times : " Lord, I am not
worthy," etc.—(St. Matt. viii., 8).

Then taking the Host in his right hand, he
communicates himself, saying : " May
the Body of Our Lord Jesus Christ preserve my soul unto life everlasting."

He then collects with the paten any particles of Host which may be left on the
corporal, and places them in the Chalice.

He receives the Precious Blood with
the particles, and then communicates the
Faithful.

The Communion of the Priest completes the
Sacrifice. It can never be omitted, and
if a Priest were suddenly taken ill another Priest must finish the Mass, even if
he is not fasting.

2 *The Ablutions.*—These are wine and water
poured into the Chalice so as to make
sure that the Priest receives every portion of the Sacred Host, and every drop

of the Precious Blood which may have clung to the Chalice.

3 *The Priest's Thanksgiving.*—The Communion and Post-Communion.

The first is an antiphon, the second is a prayer which ends the Mass; the Priest says after each: "The Lord be with you," and the server answers for the Congregation: "And with thy spirit."

4 *The offering of the Mass just said.*—This is a prayer made by the Priest, bowed down before the Altar, in which he begs God that the Sacrifice which he has offered may be acceptable for him and for all those for whom he has offered it.

Then he kisses the Altar and pronounces the blessing over the people.

5 *The Last Gospel.*—*i.e.*, the first 14 verses of the first Chapter of St. John's Gospel, except when the Rubrics prescribe another Gospel to be read instead.

How to hear Mass.

1 We can follow the Priest in the Ordinary of the Mass.

2 We can follow the Gospel story of the Passion, connecting it with the different parts of the Mass, *e.g.* :—

i. *The Priest at the foot of the Altar.*—Our Lord at the beginning of His

Passion prayed prostrate on the ground in His Agony of the Garden.

ii. *The Priest kisses the Altar.*—Judas kissed Our Lord as a traitor.

iii. *From here till the Creed.*—The Priest passes from one side of the Altar back to the middle, etc. So did Our Lord pass from Annas to Caiphas, on to Pilate, to Herod, back to Pilate.

iv. *At the Offertory: the Priest uncovers the Chalice.* Our Lord was stripped of his garments. Pilate washes his hands. Our Lord was scourged and crowned with thorns.

v. *The Priest begs the Brethren to pray* that his sacrifice and theirs may be acceptable. Our Lord exhorted the Women on His road to Calvary to pray.

vi. *The Preface and the Canon.*—Our Lord on Calvary : He is nailed to the Cross.

vii. *The Consecration.*—Our Lord is lifted up on His Cross. The two separate Consecrations represent His death, through the shedding of His Blood.

viii. *The Pater Noster.*—Our Lord's Seven Words on the Cross.

ix. *The Agnus Dei*—at which the Priest

strikes his breast. So too the Centurion : " Indeed this was the Son of God."

x. *The Priest's Communion.*—Our Lord's Death : His Body is taken down from the Cross by Joseph of Arimathea, and laid in His Mother's arms.

xi. *The end of Mass.*—Our Lord is laid in the Tomb.

3 *We can make a picture in our mind of each of the 14 Stations* of the Cross, and connect them with the different parts of the Mass; or, if we like, we can do the same with Our Lady's Seven Dolours; or with Our Lord's Seven Last Words.

4 *We can say our Rosary,* especially the Sorrowful Mysteries.

Invite the children to vary their way of hearing Mass, sometimes taking one way, sometimes another.

Interest is a vital point here as elsewhere.

Remind them that every Mass should include Communion—if not Sacramental, then Spiritual—*e.g.* :—

" My Lord Jesus Christ, I long with my whole heart to be united to Thee now and for ever."

(Pope's Catechism, p. 154).

M

SECTION VI.

The Church

The Communion of Saints.

Our Lord came on earth for a twofold purpose :

(*a*) To redeem the world.

(*b*) To found His Church.

When He hung on the Cross in death, He redeemed the world. When He was training and instructing His Apostles, He was founding His Church.

This work of His was not ready-made :

He founded it during His life-time.

At His Ascension, He left the Foundation Stones only : His Blessed Mother and His Apostles.

Then He sent the Holy Ghost to be Its Life, and to build up with Him by degrees " a glorious Church, without spot or wrinkle or any such thing."

Let us see first the general Plan of this great Work of Christ, the Church:

This Church of God is made up of living stones—souls, destined to live for ever. Most of these souls pass through three stages:

The first is their life on earth:

Here they learn about God: the Incarnation—Redemption—Heaven—and they possess (through Baptism) Sanctifying Grace in their souls. This is increased through life by the Sacraments, prayers and good works.

This first stage is a difficult one, and to keep Sanctifying Grace in their soul, they have to fight, and are, as you know, through Confirmation, Soldiers of Christ.

Therefore it is said that they belong to the Church *militant*—(connect "military").

Then death comes, and their souls, separated from their bodies, pass, in most cases, through the second stage—spent in Purgatory.

Here the souls, full of Sanctifying Grace and most pleasing to God, pay, in pain, the debt they owe to Him—they belong to *the Church Suffering*—the same Church as the Church militant, only the second stage, as it were, in It.

The third stage begins when the glorious moment of their release from Purgatory comes, and they join the other blessed Spirits in Heaven, before the Throne of God : their souls are full of Sanctifying Grace, and their debts are paid.

They have triumphed over the devil, the World, and the Flesh, enjoy Our Lord's Triumph, and so they are said to belong to the *Church Triumphant.*

In all three stages the soul lives the supernatural life, owing to the Sanctifying Grace within, and Sanctifying Grace is the great link which binds all three stages together.

They are all three united in Our Blessed Lord, Whose members they are.

They all three meet in the Holy Sacrifice of the Mass, offered on earth, and at which the Holy Souls in Purgatory and the Saints in Heaven assist.

There is another bond of union, and that is the constant communication between the three stages, and the sharing of all good things :

On earth.—Prayer for one another and help given to one another ; doing also what we can for the souls in Purgatory, and praise and honour to the Saints.

In Purgatory the Holy Souls get the benefit of the Masses and prayers of those on earth, and pay them back in prayer and help when they get to Heaven.

In Heaven we pray for and help the souls

in Purgatory, and also the souls on earth.

So that there is a constant, unceasing intercourse between the three states—all united as we are under our one Head—Jesus Christ.

When Our Lord looks down on His Church, He sees us on earth, fighting our battle and not yet sure of victory. He sees too that dark land of Purgatory, of which on earth we know very little, but which we do know is full of pain and sorrow; and then He sees the crown of His great Work, the bright Heaven, where the Church triumphs, and where we shall, please God, some day triumph too.

You might think for a moment, too, of *Grace*.

Grace is the uniting force which makes the Church militant, Suffering, and Triumphant, *One*.

You might look on it as a mighty river running down the slopes of Calvary, red with Our Lord's Precious Blood, coursing in innumerable channels all over the earth and bearing countless souls on its waters, till at last it carries them to Purgatory, where all seems dark and dreary, save for the flames which light it up. But the river is going on its way surely, steadily, and it bears the souls along, with no fear now of shipwreck, till at last it bursts forth a glorious stream, carrying the purified souls to Heaven.

The Four Marks of the Church.

The children will already know a great deal of this matter.   The following points should be brought home or revised :—

1 The True Church of God on earth must be a *Visible Body:*

  (a) Because Christ so founded It.   Its Rulers and its subjects are both visible : the Shepherd, the Sheep and the Lambs—these can be seen.

  (b) The services, ceremonies, etc., are visible.   Holy Mass is a Sacrifice you can see and hear.   In each of the Sacraments there is, as you know, an Outward Sign.

  (c) "As the Father hath sent Me, I also send you."
    The Pope who is, as St. Catherine of Siena says, the Christ on earth, does the same : He sends His Bishops and Priests all over the world to preach the Gospel.   This again can be seen. Therefore the *Church is Visible.*

2 When a beautiful Cathedral is built we see the *result:* we do not see the planning, calculations, labour, etc., which were used in building it :

So with the Church of God : we see the *result:* we do not see the Holy Ghost (for He is a Spirit) working in the Church, sanctifying souls, chiefly through the Sacraments and Holy Sacrifice, and by His Inspirations, giving Faith, Hope and Charity to the members of the Church, etc.

That which gives life to the body we call the soul. He Who gives the Church Her Life, *i.e.*, the Holy Ghost, is called Her Soul.

The Soul and the Body form one Church : just as the human soul and body form one man.

The Church therefore is visible : now, to be visible is one thing, to be recognisable is another.

Supposing someone terribly disfigured by illness, or someone who puts on a clever disguise : they would be visible, but they might not be recognisable. False Churches are visible too : the point is—The Church of God must be so marked that all may be able to recognise Her, *as* the Church of God.

And, as you know, She has four big marks on Her which are unmistakable :—

Unity—

There is but one true Church, since Christ founded but one.

"On *this* rock " (not rocks) : thus obviously all others must be contrary to His Will.

" I will build *My Church* " (not churches).

On Peter : on one man—therefore no other man will do. The Church is to have one Head, not many.

The Church is *one* Sheepfold, and in *One Fold*—there is but *One Shepherd.*

" Go ye and teach *all* nations." Since all nations are to be taught by Peter's Church, there is no work left for other churches.

"¡ One body and one Spirit : as you are called in one hope of your calling : one Lord : one Faith : one Baptism : one God and Father of all."—(Eph. iv., 4-6).

"As there are many rays of light, but one sun, many branches but one root, many streams but one source, so the Church sends forth Her rays over the whole earth, yet the light is one and its unity is undivided."—(St. Cyprian).

Holiness—

She is holy in Her divine origin ; in Her object ; holy in Her children ; in the means of holiness (Doctrine, Sacraments, Sacrifice), holy in Her union with Christ.

She has always had Saints and will always have them, because God gives the members of the Church *everything* to make them holy. *Some* are sure to let these means do their work, and these will be Saints—God's Tools never fail.

Unusual gifts of God are a proof of holiness : *e.g.*, miracles, prophecies, etc.—these are found in the true Church alone. They have been found there in all ages, and are still found there to-day : *e.g.*, Lourdes : miracles attested in the process of every canonisation, etc.

False Churches not only have not got them, but even try to deny the possibility of such things.

Thus Our Lord's promise is fulfilled. (See John xiv., 12, and Mark xvi., 17).

This mark of holiness does not mean that *all* Catholics are holy—they are not : each one can refuse to be holy and many do. Our Lord said that even up to the end there would be cockle in the wheat, and bad fish among the good.—(Matt. xiii., 26 and 49).

Catholic—

In time: " I am with you *all days*."

In doctrine: " Teach them *all things*, whatsoever I have commanded you."

With regard to all men: " Teach ye *all nations* "; " preach to every creature."—(Mark xvi., 15).

In place: " Go ye into the *whole World*.—(Matt. xxviii., 19).

" Wheresoever this Gospel shall be preached in *the whole world*, that also which she hath

done, shall be told for a memory of her."—
(Matt. xxvi., 13).

" You shall be witnesses unto Me in Jerusalem and in all Judea and Samaria, and *even
to the uttermost parts of the earth*."—(Acts
i., 8).

This being so, how can a National Church
be true ?

> *Apostolic*—
>
> *(a)* In its gifts : *i.e.*, in what it received
>   from the Apostles (doctrines, Sacra-
>   ments, Sacrifice, etc.).
>
> *(b)* In the way it is governed—just the
>   same way as Christ told His Apostles
>   He wished it to be.
>
> *(c)* In the succession of its Rulers.—(See
>   p. 92).

This last is a pure historical fact, the truth
of which there is no denying, and therefore
forming one of the four *Marks* of the Church—
a visible thing which anyone can see.

At the Last Day, when Our Lord appears
to judge all men, He will stand as the Head
of the Church; its members will be all
gathered round Him; there will be only one
Fold and one Shepherd, and these four Marks
will then shine in their full glory.

In life, they are like four beautiful stars to
guide us on our way; then after death we

shall see how they have led us to the very
Throne of God.

THE ENDOWMENTS OF THE CHURCH.

We read in St. Matthew xxii., 2, that the
Kingdom of Heaven is like to a King who
made a marriage for his son.

We may liken the King to God the Father:
His Son, therefore, is Our Lord Jesus Christ.
He, when on earth, called Himself the Bride-
groom, and His Bride is the Church.

Our Lord, like a royal Bridegroom, gave
His Church rich presents called *endowments*
(cf. " dowry "), which She has carefully kept,
and will keep till the end of time.—(See Acts
xx., 28).

The first of these great gifts or Endowments
      is :

Authority in Ruling.—The Authority of the
      Church is the Authority of God.

Jesus Christ founded the Church, and Jesus
Christ is God.

To rebel against this Authority of the
Church in ruling is to commit the sin of
Schism.

Now this Authority is threefold :

First as Teacher.—By which the Church tells
      us what Christ has revealed, and She is,
      as you know, an infallible Teacher, that

is, when teaching us, She cannot make a mistake.

Second as Priest.—By which She offers up the Holy Sacrifice and gives us the Sacraments.

Third, as Shepherd or Pastor of our souls, by which She guides us to Heaven.

Jesus Christ gave His own Authority to the Church : " He that heareth *You* heareth *Me.*"

What the Church says, *I* (God) say.

The Voice of the Church is the Voice of God : there is no difference as far as Authority is concerned.

Authority may be exercised in two ways : *(a)* direct; *(b)* indirect—*e.g.*, your father may himself order you to do something, or he may send your elder brother to tell you, from him, to do it.

If in this second case you disobey your brother, it is in reality an act of disobedience to your father, and he will treat it as such.

Therefore when the Church tells us anything about what we have to believe or to do, if we disobey Her, we disobey God, and Our Lord spoke very severely about those who disobey Him through the Church—He called them heathens and publicans.

Second Endowment: Indefectibility in Existence.—

This long word simply means : will endure or last to the end of time.

The *Rock* of Peter.—A rock in the sea remains firm and unshaken, never mind how strong the waves : the *wave* gets broken and dashed back—the rock does not move—so of the Church and Her enemies.

What Christ has Himself made could only fail and come to an end *if He willed it to;* but He has distinctly told us that He wills it to last throughout all ages : " The Gates of Hell shall *not* prevail against it."—(Matt xvi., 18).

" *I* am with you."—(Matt. xxviii., 20).

The end of the Church (the salvation of souls) is a perpetual one, for there will always be souls to save, and until its end is accomplished, *i.e.,* until the Last Day, the Church Militant will endure.

Third Endowment: Infallibility.—When the Church tells us what to believe, what to disbelieve, what is right to do, and what is wrong, She cannot make a mistake; and this is Her third great Endowment.

Again She cannot fail in Her end, but if She led us astray She would fail in it, therefore God will not allow Her to lead us astray.

Infallibility does not enable the Church to teach us *new* truths, not yet revealed. Revelation stopped at the death of the last Apostle. Our Lord then left to His Church, *all* that He wished Her to teach, and in that teaching He is with Her, and so She cannot go wrong. The Spirit of Truth abides with Her for ever. —(See John xiv., 17).

Help children to explain :

> The Church is "the pillar and ground of Truth."—(1 Tim., iii., 15).
>
> "It hath pleased the Holy Ghost and us."—(Acts xv., 18).

The Fathers of the Church call the decrees of the General Councils "God's own Word." *General Councils*—*i.e.*, one to which all Bishops have been summoned; which is presided over by the Pope in person, or by his Legate, and at which a number of Bishops actually attend, sufficient to represent the Teaching Body of the Church.

Those who are not present, give their consent tacitly.

The Church exercises Her gift of Infallibility by Her Councils.

When the Pope and Bishops (though not assembled) agree to some matter of Faith or morals, this decision is also infallible.

The ordinary and daily preaching of Christian Doctrine throughout the Church is also infallible.

And finally, the Pope Himself, speaking from the Chair of Peter (ex Cathedra) is infallible.

From the Council of Nice (A.D. 325; at

which Arius, who denied that Our Lord was
truly God, was condemned) to the Vatican
Council opened on December 8th, 1869, by
Pius IX. (at which the doctrine of the Infallibility of the Pope was defined), there have
been 20 General Councils. The Vatican Council was never closed because Rome was cap-
tured in 1870 by the Italian troops.

The Pope is guarded from all error by God
Himself; that is why in matters of faith and
of right and wrong, he cannot make a mistake; it is by God's help, not by any quality
in him.

And of course it follows: If the Pope is
our infallible Teacher we are bound to believe.

If He is our infallible Guide, we are bound
to follow his guidance.

If Peter is to feed the Sheep and the Lambs,
they are bound to accept the spiritual food
he gives them.

The Holy Father, like St. Peter, has
supreme and absolute power, coming directly
and immediately from Our Lord. He is the
one, living Apostle, who gets his powers
directly from Christ.

He is called and he is the Bishop of Rome,
because he and he alone has succeeded to the
Chair of Peter.

So too, he is called "Holy Father,"
"Supreme Pontiff."

"Bishop of Bishops."—(Tertullian).

" The Archbishop of all the Churches."—
(St. Irenaeus).

" The Most Holy and *Universal* Archbishop
and Patriarch of Great Rome."—(Council of
Chalcedon, A.D. 451).

" The Roman Pontiff . . . Vicar of Christ,
Head of the whole Church and the Father and
Teacher of all Christians."—(Council of Flor-
ence, A.D. 1459).

A few details concerning a Papal Election
will interest the children, and make the picture of the Pope more living in their minds.

Some are given here for the Teacher's
convenience :—

A Novena of Funeral Services is first made
for the deceased Pontiff, after which the Conclave opens.

The first six days of the Novena, the Service is carried on by the Canons of St. Peter's ;
the last three, it is held in the Sixtine Chapel,
by the Cardinals themselves.

At the opening of the Conclave, a solemn
votive Mass of the Holy Ghost is sung. There
are no signs of mourning, except that the Cardinals still wear their purple.

A Governor and a Marshal see to the clos-
ing in of all openings, and they have to swear
on oath that the enclosure is walled up, and

that the entrance door is locked with three keys.

This enclosure is not a mere figure of speech : the Cardinals are absolutely cut off from all communication with the outside world, and if any letters have to be delivered, they pass first through the hands of the Censor.

The Cardinal's rooms are assigned to them by lot, and they take their places at table just as they happen to arrive. The Cardinal Dean presides. The food is of the simplest.

The Votive Mass of the Holy Ghost, Litany of Our Lady, and the " We fly to Thy Patronage," precede each morning meeting. At this Mass those of the Cardinals who wish, communicate, the others say Mass in private.

There are two meetings each day, and two votings at each meeting.

Each Cardinal has a seat, and a little table in front of him. A large table is in the middle; at the head of the Assembly an Altar, a large Crucifix and six large candles alit.

Three Cardinals take up the votes and proclaim results; three Supervisors are attached to these.

The Cardinals advance in single file, the eldest first. When they reach the Altar, they

N

genuflect, kneel in prayer for a moment, then read aloud the oath :

> " I take Christ Our Lord, Who will be my
> Judge to witness, that I choose the one,
> whom, before God, I believe I ought
> to choose."

He then places his sealed vote on a Paten, slips it into the Chalice placed upon the Altar, bows to the Crucifix and retires.

The votes are burnt after each result has been read aloud ; a handful of straw and flax is burnt with the papers if no Election has been made, so that the people watching outside see *black* smoke ascending.

It requires two-thirds of the Votes of the Sacred College for an Election.

After the Pope has been elected, the Cardinals gather round him in concentric circles, and the Cardinal Dean asks him if he accepts :

After two minutes pause, Cardinal Ratti, afterwards Pius XI., answered : " Lest I should seem not fully to adhere to the divine Will, lest I should seem to withdraw from the burden thus placed upon my shoulders, lest I should seem to make little account of your Eminences' wishes, in spite of my indignity, of which I am conscious, I accept."

The next question is : " By what name do you wish to be called ?"

When the Elect Pope has answered, each

of the Cardinals salutes him in turn; he retires
to don the white cassock, and on his return,
in the presence of all, the Cardinal Dean
puts the Ring of the Fisherman on to his
finger.

Then he receives the homage of each Cardinal : *i.e.*, the kissing of the feet and of the
Ring.

The first Cardinal of the Order of Deacons
announces from the Balcony of St. Peter's :

> " I bring you tidings of great joy: we
> have a Pope, the Most Eminent and
> Reverend ———————— who has taken
> the name of ————————"

The second homage is paid by the Cardinals
in the afternoon, before the Conclave breaks
up; the third, the next day, and for this the
violet sign of mourning is laid aside.

At the Coronation the Pope himself sings
the Mass; he is carried from the Altar to the
Throne (about 60 yards apart), each time the
Ritual requires it, during Mass, and each
time, he blesses the crowds as he passes.

Devotion to the Sacred Heart

Revise what the children already know with
regard to this devotion.

I.—Teach the dogma on which the devotion
rests : namely, the Hypostatic Union.   This

means the union of the divine and human
natures in the Person of Jesus Christ.

The word " Hypostatic " means personal.

Teach the invocation : " Heart of Jesus,
hypostatically united to the Word of God,
have mercy on us."

Because of the Hypostatic Union, we *adore*
the Heart of Our Blessed Lord and love it,
but, of course, in devotion to the Sacred
Heart, it is really the Person of Our Lord we
love : His Heart is the seat and the symbol
of His love.

We do not tell our friends that we love their
heart, but that we love themselves, and it is
the same with Our Lord, but we do tell, both
Him and them, that we love with all our
heart, or heartily, as the case may be.

And Our Lord loves us with all His Heart,
too.

Our Lady was the first lover of the Sacred
Heart ; then St. John and the Apostles and
St. Mary Magdalen, because they loved Our
Lord with a strong, personal love.

Many Saints before the Reformation had
devotion to the Sacred Heart : for instance—
St. Bernard, St. Gertrude, St. Mechtilde.

After the Reformation even good people
began to think less and less of Our Lord's
love, and more of His Justice and Holiness ;
and then, in the 17th century, a terrible

heresy broke out, called Jansenism, which drove many thousands of people away from God. It taught that no one was worthy to go to Holy Communion unless they led very austere lives, and that they should only go once a year.

(Recall the decree of Pius X., concerning daily Communion).

No child was allowed to make his First Communion till he was 15 or 16, though Our Lord had Himself said : " Suffer the *little* children to come unto Me."

Our Lord was deeply grieved that the people were being taught to be afraid of Him, and when He appeared to St. Margaret Mary, it was as we see Him in pictures and statues of the Sacred Heart, speaking of love and pity.

II.—Make the children find out in their New Testaments, in the discourse after the Last Supper, all the words which tell us of Our Lord's love, and what He asks of us in return.

The chief texts are as follows :

St. John xiii., verse 1.—"Having loved His own who are in the world, He loved them unto the end."

In verses 14, 15, Our Lord tells His disciples what He wants from them. Get this from the children.

St. John xiv. :—

   1 Let not your heart be troubled : you believe in God, believe also in Me.

   6 I am the Way, the Truth and the Life : No man cometh to the Father, except by Me. (Apply to the Sacred Heart).

   13 Whatsoever you ask the Father in My Name that will I do. (Boundless trust and confidence).

   15 If you love Me, keep My Commandments.

   18 I will not leave you orphans : I will come to you. (In the Blessed Sacrament, where the Sacred Heart beats for us).

   21 He that hath My Commandments and keepeth them, he it is that loveth Me.

   23 If any man love Me, He will keep My word. . . .

   24 He that loveth Me not, keepeth not My word.

In Chapter xv. get the children to pause at verses 9, 10, 11, 12, 13, 14, 17, and again in Chapter xvii., verses 24 and 26. From these, Our Lord's own words, let the children find out what they must do to practise devotion to the Sacred Heart.

III.—A lesson on St. Margaret Mary might with advantage be given, and the various acts of Reparation, given on p. 39, might be revised.

IV.—Teach that the Church has recognised two distinct spirits, in which devotion to the Sacred Heart may be practised :

The one, based on personal love of Our Lord and imitation of the virtues of His Sacred Heart is characterised by joy in His friendship, and happiness because of His invitation to abide in His love.

This spirit is shown in the Mass : " Egredimini," which, with the corresponding Office, is approved of by the Church for Ireland, Spain, Venice and for the Society of the Sacred Heart.

The other is a spirit of Reparation and Expiation, and whilst dwelling on Our Lord's suffering love, endeavours to atone for all the wounds He has received, especially in the Holy Sacrament of the Altar.

This spirit is shown in the Mass "Miserebitur."

The Proper of both Masses might be read to the children. They contain much matter from Scripture bearing on the subject.

Further lessons might be given on the Invocations of the Litany of the Sacred Heart,

also on the Saints most devoted to Its worship : *e.g.*—St. Gertrude, St. Mechtilde, St.
Madeleine Sophie.

THE END

www.ingramcontent.com/pod-product-compliance
Lightning Source LLC
Chambersburg PA
CBHW031232090426
42742CB00007B/169